B.C.

Mareh

Brooke, Z. N. (Zachary Nugent), 1883-1946.
The English church & the papacy :
from the conquest to the reign of John

THE ENGLISH CHURCH
AND THE PAPACY

LONDON
Cambridge University Press
FETTER LANE

NEW YORK · TORONTO
BOMBAY · CALCUTTA · MADRAS
Macmillan

TOKYO
Maruzen Company Ltd

THE
ENGLISH CHURCH
&
THE PAPACY

FROM
THE CONQUEST TO
THE REIGN OF
JOHN

BY

Z. N. BROOKE, M.A.

Fellow of Gonville & Caius College, Cambridge
Birkbeck Lecturer at Trinity College
Cambridge 1929–31

CAMBRIDGE
AT THE UNIVERSITY PRESS
1931

PRINTED IN GREAT BRITAIN

To
MY WIFE

CONTENTS

PREFACE

This book owes its appearance to three main causes. The desire to work out the relations of the English Church with the Papacy in the eleventh and twelfth centuries had long lain at the back of my mind, but it was only when the Council of Trinity College did me the honour of inviting me to deliver the Birkbeck Lectures during the two following academic years that I received the necessary incentive and opportunity. Then, when I took the subject in hand, it soon became evident that everything depended on determining what was the law in the English Church in the eleventh and twelfth centuries, and that only an extensive search to discover what collections of ecclesiastical law were then in existence in England could provide a solution of that problem. To make such a search among all the available libraries in England necessitated a considerable amount of leisure and lengthy absences from Cambridge, and I am indebted to my University and my College for the year's leave of absence from my ordinary duties without which I could not have properly completed the lectures, still less have prepared them without delay for publication. Thirdly, the Syndics of the University Press generously offered to undertake the publication, and I am much indebted to the invariable kindness and expert assistance of their staff.

Substantially this book reproduces the twelve lectures which I delivered in the two academic years, 1929–31. There are a few additions, and the repetitions which were necessary in a course extending over two years have of course been omitted. Some of my later discoveries have been fitted into their right place, and the lectures have been rearranged in order, so that the first part contains all the information about ecclesiastical law in England, and the historical development is treated consecutively in the second part. I have considerably revised the lectures before publication, and added the necessary references and notes, but I have not attempted to reshape them altogether. I hope that my frequent use of the first person singular, which is often necessary in addressing a visible audience, will not grate on the ear of the reader.

A search of the kind that I undertook naturally involves many calls on the time and knowledge of those who have the care of manuscripts, and I should like to take this opportunity of recording my gratitude for the generous assistance I received everywhere. In particular I wish to express my thanks to the University Librarian, the Secretary, and the assistants in Room Theta; to the librarians of Corpus Christi College, Pembroke College, Peterhouse, and Trinity College; to Dr H. H. E. Craster, Keeper of the Western Manuscripts in the Bodleian Library; to Mr A. L. Poole, Librarian of St John's College, Oxford; to the officials in the Manuscript Room of the British Museum; to the Provost of Eton College; to Canon C. Jenkins and his assistant, Dr Churchill, at Lambeth Palace Library; to Canon A. T. Bannister at Hereford; and to M. H. Omont, Conservateur du département des manuscrits, Bibliothèque Nationale, who also very kindly caused two manuscripts to be brought from Rouen to Paris for my use. Also I wish to express my thanks to the Dean and Chapter of Canterbury, Durham, Hereford, Lincoln, and Salisbury cathedrals, all of whom allowed manuscripts to be sent to the Cambridge University Library for my use.

I have attempted to denote in the text my obligations to those writers whose books have helped me in my work. Two of these need particular mention. In Part I I have been especially indebted to M. Paul Fournier, as every student of the history of pre-Gratian canon law must be. His definitive *Histoire des collections canoniques du faux Isidore à Gratian*, written in collaboration with Professor G. Le Bras, is in the Press as I write, so that I am unable to give references to it. I had the privilege of discussing my work with M. Fournier in January last, and of showing him a list of the English manuscripts which I had found. He very kindly allowed me to say that he fully agreed with the conclusions I had drawn from them as to canon law in England. In Part II I have made considerable use of Heinrich Böhmer's works on English Church history in the eleventh and early twelfth centuries. Though in the following pages I often express disagreement with his conclusions, especially when they were based on manuscript evidence, I am none the less considerably in his debt. He blazed a trail which has made the way much easier for his successors.

I have received assistance of another kind from those friends who have allowed me to discuss with them various problems connected with the subject of this book. I have derived no little advantage from these discussions, and in particular I wish to record my gratitude to two of these friends—Mr G. T. Lapsley of Trinity College and Dr C. W. Previté-Orton of St John's College.

Finally, to my wife I owe much for her constant encouragement and for her assistance, particularly in the drudgery of copying and indexing, in the latter of which my eldest son also had a share.

Many people, therefore, have contributed with their help to the making of this book. But for all the views expressed in it I am alone responsible, and for all its mistakes I only am to blame. I hope that it will not prove altogether unworthy of all the generous assistance that its author has received.

Z. N. BROOKE

September, 1931

INTRODUCTION

CHAPTER I

ECCLESIA ANGLICANA

THERE is a natural tendency to isolate periods and subjects in history, for the individual writer is anxious to give a unity to his theme. The result may be somewhat misleading, and not only in biographies, since the setting is often as important as the picture. The history of the English Church in the Middle Ages has especially suffered from being treated thus in isolation, as if it were a subject complete in itself. There is justification for such treatment in modern times, and this has encouraged the idea that it bore a similar character in the Middle Ages also. Sometimes its history is told as part of the general history of England, and of course any history of England in the Middle Ages which ignored the Church would be of little value; but in this way too it tends to be isolated from its proper environment. Before its story can be told separately or as part of general English history, it needs to be depicted in its rightful setting. The history of the English Church in the Middle Ages must primarily be considered as a part of medieval Church history.

This sounds so obvious a platitude that I might well have refrained from giving utterance to it, were it not that it is just this treatment which it has never properly received. And, for this reason, when its relations with the central government of the Church and its Head, the Pope, have been discussed, the impression given is that the foreign policy and relations of the English Church are being described, its contacts with a foreign power to whose authority it is naturally not anxious to be subordinate. If this were a true view, and if such an independent position had been possible, the Church would not have been a real unity, but a federation of independent national Churches. We know that it was a real unity, and was so regarded in all its parts; this is an essential truth, to which we must adhere in spite of apparent contradictions. And if we keep it in mind and contemplate the Church from the centre out-wards, we get a very different impression of the English Church from that which is normally current.

I propose to start with the general history of the Church, and to consider to what extent the history of the English Church is consonant with and illustrated by what was happening elsewhere. Undoubtedly the most important question which arises concerns its relations with, and recognition of, the authority of the central government of the Church. It is necessary, then, in the first place, to say something of this central government and the authority that it was able, or claimed, to exercise. Secondly, it is necessary to characterise the law of the Church and its develop-ment during the eleventh and twelfth centuries. That brings us to the most important consideration of all, to discover what we can about the law which prevailed in the English Church during this period. Were the same books, the same collections, in use as elsewhere, or did the English Church, as so many people have imagined, decide for itself which of the canons of the

Roman Church it would or would not accept, and otherwise legislate for itself independently? This is an investigation which, for most of the period, has never seriously been undertaken, and to it I shall devote the First Part of this book. The Second Part will in its turn depend also on this investigation, for the historical sketch from 1066 to 1200 will especially be related to the legal situation. I shall attempt to show how far the legal and the actual conflicted, and to trace the stages which led eventually to their practical coincidence.

But, to begin with, I want to make a preliminary investigation, introductory in character, which necessitates a survey of the whole period and more particularly of the second half of the period. The purpose of this investigation is to elucidate the meaning of the phrase "the English Church", not the meaning that may attach to it to-day, but the sense in which it was used in the period of which I am speaking. It is, after all, a literal translation of *ecclesia Anglicana* which, as everybody knows, occurs in Magna Carta and was certainly in regular use afterwards; and I believe that the meaning it conveyed at that time was implicit in the minds of churchmen throughout the period with which I am concerned, though they might use other phrases to express it. And if I may appear to be tedious in spending so much time on a definition, it is a definition vital to my purpose, and one that colours all that I have to say hereafter. It will at once make clear my subject, and help to limit the range of my enquiry.

Now the phrase *ecclesia Anglicana* is one that has given rise to numerous misconceptions, because it seems to convey a significance similar to that which was given to it deliberately at a later date, especially owing to its appearance in Magna Carta. That is why I wish to begin with the Great Charter, and to note in the first place the inference which the leading authority on the Charter, Professor McKechnie, drew from the use of it in that document. He says[1]:

It is perhaps worthy of note that while the charters of Henry I and Stephen spoke only of "holy church", John speaks of the "English church". This change suggests a growth of patriotism among the prelates, led by Stephen Langton.

If he states this in a somewhat tentative form, he makes it more definite by giving to his treatment of this part of the Charter the heading "The National Church". Certainly, on the surface, his inference appears eminently reasonable, and it has been widely accepted. But, before commencing my own investigations, I should like to call attention to two preliminary, though minor, considerations, bearing on Professor McKechnie's assumption. Firstly, that Magna Carta was preceded by a charter of liberties to the Church, in which the same phrase occurs twice, and that this charter was sent to Pope Innocent III and received his confirmation; surely so keen-sighted a lawyer as that Pope would have objected to the phrase, if it were as significant as Professor McKechnie thinks. And secondly, *ex hypothesi*, we might expect the very opposite to have happened. Would it not be more

[1] *Magna Carta*, p. 224, n. 1.

natural to look for the idea of a national Church in the eleventh century, when papal authority was rigidly excluded, than in the thirteenth when it had gradually come to be recognised as the supreme authority in the Church of England? But though these considerations bear more relation to the facts than the assumption made by Professor McKechnie, they are still equally no more than assumptions. To turn, now, to something more positive. There is a danger that the reader might draw, from the reference to Stephen Langton, the further inference that the use of the phrase *ecclesia Anglicana* was a novelty, and therefore startling in its sudden emergence. That would be a grave mistake, for, as I shall show, the phrase had been in current use for at least fifty years.

But, before I come to that, I want to say something of a much earlier phrase, from which no similar inference has been drawn—*ecclesia Anglorum*. This goes right back to Gregory the Great, who used it in his letters to Augustine. Occasionally as a variant we find *ecclesia Angliae*, especially in the letters of St Anselm; he employs the same variation in speaking of the king of England, whom he always addresses correctly as "rex Anglorum" but sometimes refers to as "rex Angliae". It is quite clear what Anselm's meaning was when he used the phrase. He is not likely to be accused of a narrowly national outlook, for it was the lawfulness of papal authority which in his contests with the English kings he particularly championed. Now in a letter to Pope Paschal II,[1] speaking of the claims of York against Canterbury, he says that their

[1] Eadmer, *Historia Novorum*, ed. Rule, M., Rolls Series, p. 201.

recognition will involve a schism of the *ecclesia Angliae*. An embassy from him to the king on the same subject[1] says that the integrity of "Christianitas" would be torn asunder. While, on the other side, archbishop Thomas of York[2] asserts that they will not divide "the Church". Both of them meant the same thing, and clearly "ecclesia Angliae", "Christianitas", "ecclesia" are used as synonyms. Obviously only one part of the Church would be affected by this question. Anselm specified the part, though it was not necessary to do so. He used *ecclesia Angliae* as the natural phrase to express that part of the Church of which he claimed to be primate, just as Paschal II wrote in a letter to him, "religio tua in Anglici regni regione praesideat".[3] The more ordinary phrase, *ecclesia Anglorum*, is used by him and by others in an exactly similar sense. Though the evidence, particularly the more satisfactory evidence from letters, becomes scarce for some time after St Anselm's death, it may be taken to be a normal phrase in fairly common use. When we come to the early letters of John of Salisbury (i.e. those written before the death of archbishop Theobald in 1161), we find a number of instances of its use, especially in the letters he wrote as secretary to the archbishop, and sometimes addressed to the Pope himself.

But from that time *ecclesia Anglorum* begins to give way before the new phrase, *ecclesia Anglicana*, which gradually ousts it from general use. Already in two of

---

[1] Eadmer, *Historia Novorum*, ed. Rule, M., Rolls Series, p. 205.
[2] Quoted by Hugh the Chanter (*Historians of the Church of York*, ed. Raine, J., Rolls Series, vol. II, p. 118).
[3] Eadmer, *op. cit.* p. 135.

the early letters of John of Salisbury this has appeared[1], letters written almost certainly in 1160. When
we turn to the great Becket correspondence, edited in
three volumes of the Rolls Series by Canon Robertson, we can trace the supersession of the earlier by the
later phrase. *Ecclesia Anglorum* dominates at first
absolutely; and by this I mean that, though the writers
when speaking of the Church in England normally
simply say "ecclesia", if they do wish to be more
precise they always say "ecclesia Anglorum". Then in
1163 the Pope writing to Gilbert Foliot twice speaks
of *ecclesia Anglica*.[2] But it is the same Pope, Alexander III, who first introduces *ecclesia Anglicana* into
this correspondence, in a letter of 1165.[3] From 1166
onwards it becomes dominant, and *ecclesia Anglorum*
gradually disappears. It occasionally reappears, either
as a slip by those who had used it before but now normally use *ecclesia Anglicana*, such as Becket and John
of Salisbury; or by some who we may infer have not
learnt the new terminology, such as the writers of four
letters on behalf of Gilbert Foliot in 1169;[4] so, too, in
the life of Becket by William fitz Stephen, whereas in
the other lives *ecclesia Anglicana* is regularly used—
about twenty-five times in all. In this supersession of
one phrase by another there is no change of sense.

[1] Nos. 65 and 124. It also appears in his *Historia Pontificalis*,
c. 42 (written *c.* 1164).
[2] Vol. v, p. 62. I have only found three other instances of *ecclesia
Anglica*, all of them in the collection of Anselm's letters, though not
in letters written by himself. The writers were bishop Gundulf of
Rochester (actually "Angelica," according to Migne, but this is a
misprint), archbishop Hugh of Lyons, and Pope Paschal II (Anselm,
epp. III, 3, 124; IV, 83).
[3] Vol. v, p. 240.   [4] Vol. vi, pp. 616, 618, 624, 630.

From all the instances I have collected I am quite clear that the phrases are synonymous. They are used in exactly the same way, in collocation with the same words, and the change of phrase by such writers as Becket and John of Salisbury, coupled with their accidental reversion to the older phrase, is clearly a change of terminology and not of meaning.

The fact, and the date of the change are clear. The reason for the change is not so evident. My own conclusion is that the new phrase was adopted as being more in keeping with the normal terminology of the Roman Church to use the adjectival form.[1] Alexander III had begun with *Anglica* in 1163 and then adopted *Anglicana* in 1165. He had been anticipated in this by John of Salisbury, who had himself been a clerk in the papal curia before he became a clerk of archbishop Theobald; John wrote to the Pope himself a letter for that archbishop using this phrase, which a few years later is adopted by the Pope and then becomes the regular expression. Further, I suggest that *Anglicana* was preferred to the more normal adjective *Anglica* from the analogy of the much older expression, *ecclesia Gallicana*, which had been in common use for centuries and was certainly familiar in England. There is an early twelfth-century instance of its

[1] Pope Paschal II in one letter, and Pope Alexander III in one letter used *Anglica*; otherwise the Popes adhered to *Anglicana*. It is worth noting that in all the papal letters I have looked at (and I have mainly confined myself for this purpose to letters concerned with English affairs), I have only found one instance of a Pope using a non-adjectival form. Innocent III (Reg. v, 90) uses "ecclesia Angliae". This was perhaps natural at a time when it was becoming correct to address the king of England as "rex Angliae". Cf. also what I say later about the *Provinciale*, where English sees are put under the heading "Anglia".

use in Hugh the Chanter,[1] who was writing probably *c.* 1127. In the Becket correspondence it is quite common, in letters of Becket and other English bishops and of French bishops as well; and it is frequently coupled with *Anglicana* in the same sentence. In the earlier letters in this collection we find "Anglorum ecclesia et Gallicana", a clumsy phrase which must have grated on the sensitive ear of John of Salisbury, trained as he had been in the rhythm of the papal *cursus*. Afterwards, "Anglicana et Gallicana ecclesia(ae)" becomes the regular expression. It is significant that the earliest use of *ecclesia Anglicana*, in the letters of John of Salisbury, is in conjunction with *Gallicana*—"Alexander, quem...Anglicana et Gallicana receperunt ecclesiae". I need hardly say that *Gallicana ecclesia* in the twelfth century does not bear the connotation that it does in the later Middle Ages and in modern times. The Church in France was the first part of the Church in the eleventh century outside Italy to accept the new papal centralisation, and the phrase *Gallicana ecclesia* has certainly no nationalist implication. And this, I feel sure, is true of *Anglicana ecclesia* also.

The two phrases, the old *ecclesia Anglorum* and the new *ecclesia Anglicana*, seem, as I have said, clearly to be synonymous. In the Becket correspondence, consisting of some 800 letters, I have found *Anglorum* in 22 letters, *Anglicana* in 72, and frequently more than once in the same letter. Becket uses *Anglorum* in 4 letters, *Anglicana* in 34; John of Salisbury uses *Ang-*

---

[1] *Historians of the Church of York*, ed. Raine, J., Rolls Series, vol. II, p. 220.

lorum in 7, *Anglicana* in 19; the Pope uses *Anglicana*
in 4, *Anglorum* not at all. Both these phrases are used
almost exclusively by Becket and his supporters. The
opponents of Becket use *Anglorum* in 5 letters, *Anglicana* only in 4. This in itself is noteworthy, because,
if the phrase had a patriotic significance, it would
more naturally be found on the lips of those who
supported the king against Becket and against papal
authority. Moreover, the letters in which these
phrases occur are, as to exactly one-half of them,
addressed either to the Pope or to cardinals; *ecclesia
Anglicana* appears in 23 letters addressed to the Pope,
in 13 addressed to cardinals. At the very least it can be
said that the Roman Church had no objection to the
phrase; writers, such as John of Salisbury, knew well
what would offend the susceptibility of the Pope and
would be careful to avoid doing so. And as the Pope
uses the phrase himself, it may almost be said to have
an official ring. Further, what I suggested to be the
meaning of *ecclesia Anglorum* when used by Anselm
is clearly the meaning of *ecclesia Anglicana* as used by
Becket. Becket insists that the liberty of the *ecclesia
Anglicana* is at stake, and by liberty he makes it clear
that he means freedom from royal control, and at the
same time freedom to obey the Pope, to be governed
by papal authority as was the rest of the Church. He
is evidently asserting the right of the Church in
England to be treated in the same way that the Church
is elsewhere. The Pope when he uses the phrase uses it
in exactly the same sense. Fortunately he has supplied
us with a definition. In 1173 he wrote to cardinals
Albert and Theoduin, his legates, announcing the

canonisation of Becket, and told them that he had also written to the monks of Canterbury and to the *ecclesia Anglicana* to the same effect, and instructed them to deliver these two letters. These two letters have been preserved to us, one addressed to the monks, the other "archiepiscopis episcopis et ... aliis ecclesiarum praelatis et universo clero et populo per Angliam constitutis."[1] That is the official formal address which he abbreviates as *ecclesia Anglicana* when writing to the cardinal-legates; obviously the Pope uses *ecclesia Anglicana* to mean that part of the Church which was constituted in England.

From the Becket correspondence I pass to another great collection of letters,[2] arising from a later and lesser controversy. The monks of Christ Church, Canterbury, who formed the cathedral chapter, were in controversy with the archbishop, first Baldwin and then Hubert Walter, about the establishment of a body of secular canons, which they believed, probably with justice, to be a method of attacking both their privileges and their property. The issue dragged on from 1185 to 1201, when the monks were finally victorious, with constant appeals to Rome, where the monks kept a permanent legation during these years. In this controversy the archbishops and the king were allied against the monks and the Papacy. There are 557 letters in all, and in 31 of them the phrase *ecclesia Anglicana* occurs. Once more it is the party favoured by the Pope that mainly employs it; by the party

---

[1] Becket, *Memorials*, vol. VII, pp. 545 foll.; nos. 783, 784, 785.

[2] *Epistolae Cantuarienses*, ed. Stubbs, W., Rolls Series (Memorials etc. of Richard I, vol. II).

opposed to the convent it is only used six times. Both
sides use it in the same way; both declare that, if the
issue goes against them, it will be a disaster to the
ecclesia Anglicana; the monks add, to the *ecclesia
Romana* as well. The monks use it fifteen times, but
it is also used by two Popes, two cardinals, King
Richard I, both archbishops, and four other English
bishops, while Popes and cardinals are frequently
recipients of the letters in which it occurs. As before,
it is clearly an expression which arouses no suspicion
in Rome; as before, it is sanctioned by papal use.
Innocent III, who finally settled the question in
favour of the monks, does not in this collection (though
he does elsewhere) use the phrase *Anglicana ecclesia*,
but he does use a similar and rather remarkable expression—*Anglicana provincia*, to which I shall refer
again later. Finally, as before, we have a definition of
its meaning, this time by the archbishop of Canterbury, Hubert Walter. In March 1195, Pope Celestine
III appointed Hubert papal legate in England. He
wrote to him announcing the fact, speaking of the
Anglicana ecclesia receiving a legate of the apostolic
see. He wrote also to the archbishop of York and all
the prelates of England, stressing the plenitude of
power belonging to the Roman Church, which was
necessary for the maintenance of ecclesiastical unity,
and adding that in virtue of the duty thereby imposed
upon him he had been attentive to the needs of the
Anglicana ecclesia.[1] In the following July, Huber
Walter, while engaged in a legatine visitation of the
province of York, wrote to the monastery of St

[1] *Epistolae Cantuarienses*, pp. 368 foll.

Augustine, Canterbury, and spoke of the Pope wishing in making him legate to show his care of "hanc occidentalis ecclesiae portionem quam in Anglia plantavit Altissimus".[1] The phrase "Western Church" seems to me an unusual one, but I cannot dwell on that here. What I want to emphasise is the way in which Hubert Walter paraphrases what the Pope had spoken of as *Anglicana ecclesia*—"that portion of the Western Church which the Most High has planted in England". It is the Pope and not the archbishop who seems to be "the patriotic Englishman"! Or rather, is it not obvious that they both mean the same thing, the same too that Alexander III meant in 1173?

I have given sufficient instances, and it would be tedious to multiply them further. I have collected about 150 in all, from the fifty years preceding Magna Carta, and I expect that a still larger number could be discovered. At any rate, I have said enough to establish its frequency as a phrase in common use, and one quite normal in Roman circles. I would go further than this and suggest that its use was not merely accepted by the Pope but was in a sense initiated by him. I suggested above that possibly Roman usage was responsible at the beginning, combined with the analogy of *Gallicana*, for the change from *Anglorum* to *Anglicana*; I have shown that it was first employed by the person in England most familiar with Roman usage, John of Salisbury, and that the second person to use it was the Pope himself. It seems at first sight a paradox to suggest that the adoption of the phrase *ecclesia Anglicana* is not an indication that the Church

[1] *Ib.* p. 370.

in England is beginning to go its own way, but rather that it is beginning to go the way of the Pope; that it is following a nomenclature adopted by the Papacy in the work of ecclesiastical administration, and not one that marks its own national sense. But is it really so extraordinary that the Popes should adopt this nomenclature? Is it strange that they should consider the area they have to govern geographically according to its secular divisions? It was in some measure inevitable that they should do so. In the great task of ecclesiastical organisation, and particularly of the centralisation of the Church under papal control, the Popes had paid particular heed to the geographical and political divisions of Europe. They had acted through legates, equipped with full powers, who had been sent not merely to a province and an archbishop, but to a kingdom, itself ecclesiastically a collection of provinces. The ecclesiastical grouping had been based on the administrative divisions of the Empire in the first place; and still the ecclesiastical and secular boundaries almost always coincided. When they did not, as in the case of Lyons, the reason was due to a political and not to an ecclesiastical re-grouping; and it gave rise to considerable difficulties and often to administrative confusion. So it was not remarkable that the Popes should adopt the political group as a unit to which to send their ecclesiastical instructions; and such a course was further dictated to them by necessity. It was necessary for them to treat with the secular ruler when they wished to obtain obedience from bishops, for the bishops everywhere were bound by firm ties to the kings. The authority exercised by

a secular ruler over ecclesiastical affairs and over the
ecclesiastical officials in his kingdom made it necessary
for the Pope to deal with the Church in each kingdom
as a whole; to treat it in a sense as a single unit, and
so to give it a distinctive title.

Now that word of many meanings, "ecclesia", can
be applied both to the whole Church or to any part of
it, a province, a diocese, a parish, and it can be employed to include all Christian people within the
whole or the part, or to include only the ordained
clergy; I am not concerned here with its use when
applied to a particular building. It is sometimes clear
in which sense it is to be taken; but when, as commonly, it is necessary to be more explicit, an adjective
supplies the necessary definition—*ecclesia Londin-
iensis*, *ecclesia Cantuariensis*, *ecclesia Romana*, and so
on. Often we find these various uses combined together in one sentence; thus the monks of Canterbury,
writing to cardinal Melior, extol him for his constancy
"pro Cantuariensi, sed et pro Anglicana, sed pro
Romana et universali ecclesia".[1] How, then, when the
Pope is considering the Church in a particular kingdom will he define it other than by applying the
adjective which represents that kingdom? So far I
have only adduced two instances of this, *Gallicana* and
Anglicana. But when Clement III in 1188 and
Celestine III in 1192 write that the Church in Scotland
is dependent directly on the Roman Church, they
both speak of it as *ecclesia Scoticana*,[2] and Innocent III

---

[1] *Epistolae Cantuarienses*, ed. Stubbs, W., Rolls Series, p. 120.
[2] Clement's letter is in Migne, PL. CCIV, col. 1318, Celestine's in
Migne, PL. CCVI, col. 921.

in a most interesting letter about the Church in Ireland refers to it as *Hibernicana ecclesia*.[1] I am only quoting from letters addressed to this country. Professor J. C. Ayer[2] quotes similar usages for other countries in the thirteenth century—*ecclesia Daciana* for Denmark, *ecclesia Hungarica* for Hungary, *ecclesia Marrochitana* for the Christian population in Morocco, and I am sure that a careful search through papal letters would reveal numerous instances. There is a further proof, too, that the Papacy thought in terms of geographical and political, as well as of ecclesiastical, divisions of the Church. For instance, a collection of ecclesiastical law, especially the False Decretals, will have attached to it a list of the political divisions of the Roman Empire—"Nomina XI regionum continentium infra se provintias CXIII". In the twelfth century the need of a *Provinciale* was much greater, and it had to be up-to-date and represent the political divisions of the time. There is a good example of such a *Provinciale* attached to the work of cardinal Albinus in 1188–9, and a similar list was used by Cencius (later Pope Honorius III) in his *Liber Censuum*, or list of the sources of papal revenue, in 1192.[3] In both of them the division is first of all into kingdoms, and the kingdoms are then further subdivided into ecclesiastical provinces, and the provinces into bishoprics. In Cencius' list, England, Wales, Scotland, and Ireland are given as four separate kingdoms—and, though I

[1] Reg. v. 83.
[2] *On the Medieval National Church* (Papers of the American Society of Church History, 2nd series, vol. IV, pp. 41–75).
[3] Cf. Poole, R. L., *The Papal Chancery*, Appendix 6.

have not discovered an instance for Wales, I have
shown Popes using *ecclesia Anglicana*, *Scoticana*,
Hibernicana. Possibly it is this system of grouping
which led Innocent III to speak, as I mentioned above,
of *Anglicana provincia*. At any rate, the system of
grouping by kingdoms is clearly a normal method in an
official papal document.

Moreover, it is a commonplace to say that the
English Church in the Middle Ages was composed of
two provinces each with a separate convocation, and
that the whole Church did not meet together to act
officially as a united body except when summoned by
a papal legate. It was, in fact, the Papacy that gave
the English Church a sense of ecclesiastical unity.
And this liberty which the English Church was granted
by John in Magna Carta was liberty from royal interference, not liberty from papal control; rather, as with
Becket, it implied liberty to be under papal control.
Professor McKechnie raises the question whether the
clause in Magna Carta was meant to imply liberty
against the Pope as well as against the king; he suggests that it was so meant, though he dismisses the
question as one of merely academic interest. But
surely it is of more than academic importance, and
Professor McKechnie seems to have been led into an
illogical position by his assumption of a patriotic
implication in the phrase *ecclesia Anglicana*. How
could the king's charter grant freedom from papal
control? That would have needed a papal charter. And
how could the nobles, lay and ecclesiastical, imagine
that by this clause they could secure a double liberty
for the English Church? Already it had received

Innocent III's blessing, when sent to him in the charter of liberties for the English Church. It did exactly what he wanted; it gave freedom of canonical election to the English Church. In other words it allowed the English Church to be controlled in the matter of elections as the Church as a whole was, by the canon law of the Church. Can anyone think that it was desired to prevent the Pope from controlling elections? This would be a grave anachronism. The fact is that Professor McKechnie has misunderstood what the claim for "the freedom of the English Church" really was. From the reign of Stephen onwards it always meant the same thing, as I shall have occasion to show later. There is no question what Becket meant; he stated so very clearly that he wished to be free to obey the Pope. And it makes no sense at all if *ecclesia Anglicana* is given a patriotic and national implication.

This brings me back to the point from which I started. If I cannot accept the view that the change from *ecclesia* in the charters of Henry I and Stephen to *ecclesia Anglicana* in Magna Carta represents a growth of patriotic feeling, what then is the explanation? I doubt if an explanation is really required, for to my mind the two phrases are synonymous. When you are speaking of the Church in a particular part of the world, in this case England, you will mean exactly the same if you say "the Church" or "the Church in England". I have quoted a large number of instances of *ecclesia Anglicana*, but I could give a far larger number of instances where the same writers, in exactly similar contexts, used the single word *ecclesia*, it being perfectly clear that it was the Church in England of which they were talking. Two examples will show this. Becket, who uses the phrase more frequently than anybody, is continually harping on the theme that he is defending the liberty of the Church against Henry II; sometimes he says *ecclesia*, sometimes *ecclesia Anglicana*. There is no distinguishable difference of meaning between the two expressions in his mouth; and it is clear that it was always the Church in England that in these passages he claimed to be defending. Again, there are a large number of letters of John of Salisbury, written when he was in exile to various people in England, about the year 1167, in all of which he extols Becket as the champion of the Church; the phrases vary, but they amount to the same thing. In some of them he writes *ecclesia*, in others *ecclesia Anglicana*, and clearly there is no difference in meaning. Now, let us just review again the series of royal promises, but, for the sake of completeness, including one or two that Professor McKechnie did not mention. Henry I said "sanctam Dei ecclesiam", Stephen "sanctam ecclesiam". In both cases they were giving a charter to their subjects in England, therefore it was the Church in England to which they were referring. They might have said "ecclesiam Anglorum"[1] ("Anglicanam" was as yet unknown), but it would have made no difference. Henry II in his coronation oath, as a monk of Grandmont wrote to remind him in 1171 after Becket's death, promised and professed law, justice, and peace "ecclesiae Dei

---

[1] Actually I have not found *ecclesia Anglorum* ever used by a king, though both Henry II and Richard I used *Anglicana*.

populoque mihi subiecto".[1] In 1173, when he had
been reconciled with the Pope again, he wrote to him:
"liberam electionem *ecclesiae Anglicanae* annuimus".[2]
This is the particular liberty which was granted to the
Church by John both in November 1214 and again in
the Great Charter—freedom of election. When Henry
II used the phrase in the same connection, it cannot be
said that it denoted a growth of English patriotism in
the cardinals who persuaded him to this concession;
why then should it in Stephen Langton and the bishops
who compelled John to the same concession in 1214
and 1215?

I am of course only considering the question as far
as Magna Carta. As national feeling grew, as hostility
to the abuses of papal government increased, a different tinge of meaning may perhaps be read into the
use of *ecclesia Anglicana*, just as, at the end of the
Middle Ages, *ecclesia Gallicana* conveyed a new implication. Even so, it is only the Reformation that really
altered the whole meaning of the phrase; by the
Tudors it was deliberately given the particular significance that it now bears. I am concerned solely with
its meaning in the eleventh and twelfth centuries, and
when I speak of the English Church, I am merely
using a literal translation of *Anglicana ecclesia*. I am
content to employ the definition of this given by
Alexander III—"the archbishops, bishops and other
prelates, and all the clergy and people constituted in
England", though commonly it must be limited by

---

[1] *Materials for the History of Archbishop Thomas Becket*, ed.
Robertson, J. C., Rolls Series, vol. VII, p. 452.
[2] *Ib.* p. 553.

leaving out "the people", and sometimes also "the clergy" as well. Equally am I content with the definition supplied by archbishop Hubert Walter— "that portion of the Western Church which the Most High has planted in England". It is that portion of the Church, and its relations with the Papacy, with which I am concerned in this book.

Note. After the above was in print, I discovered that I had been quoting from Professor McKechnie's 1st edition of 1905, and not from the revised edition of 1914. In this (pp. 190 foll.), though he has revised the wording, the point remains the same and is even made more definite. So, on p. 192 he says: "the phrase ["the liberty of the English Church"] had thus an anti-papal as well as an anti-monarchical bearing."

CHAPTER II

THE WESTERN CHURCH IN THE ELEVENTH CENTURY

I HAVE made it sufficiently evident that, when I speak of the English Church, I understand the phrase to connote nothing more than that part of the Church which was constituted in England. I do not deny that it had a certain definite unity of its own, since the Papacy, by adopting this territorial nomenclature, recognised it as a constituent part of the whole Church. But we must be careful to appreciate the character of this unity, and not to attribute to it something that it only acquired at a much later date. The unity was of a secular and not of an ecclesiastical character, and was only an expression of the fact that all its members were the subjects of one king. So, too, the Norman Church had a distinct unity, in that all its members were the subjects of one duke. The fact that king and duke were the same man did not unite the two Churches. Secular conditions, which gave each Church its unity, kept the two Churches separate, even though the Norman Church supplied the English with most of its bishops and abbots; they ceased to be members of the Norman and became members of the English Church. Elsewhere this is equally true. We can speak of the German Church or the French Church (of which the Norman was in a sense a part) to imply that part of the Church situated in the territories ruled by the king of Germany or the

king of France. And, as I have said, the control of the
lay rulers over the Church in their dominions was
such that the Popes could not ignore it; accordingly,
when they sent out legates, especially standing legates,
they commonly allocated as their sphere a whole
kingdom; they sent them to Germany, to France, or
to England.

However, these divisions, though used for ecclesiastical purposes, were really only secular. Ecclesiastically, the Church was a unity, "the undivided
garment of Christ", divided for purposes of administration into provinces and sees; and its provinces did
not always coincide with the secular divisions. In the
eleventh century there was nobody in England, or
elsewhere, who questioned the essential unity of the
Church, or denied that it was under papal headship.
This is certainly true of England after the Conquest,
when William I brought the English Church back again
into line with the Church as a whole, and it is for this
reason that I have chosen the Conquest as the point
from which to commence this enquiry. The Conquest
does mark, in essentials, such a clean sweep with the
past. Not only the new secular ruler, but also the
new ecclesiastical officials, came from the Continent.
During Edward the Confessor's reign, foreigners had
been introduced, but there was great hostility to them.
Now they are imposed without effective resistance
everywhere, and it is some time before an Englishman
has a chance of promotion in the English Church. It
is particularly the Church that is affected by one of
the principal results of the Conquest—the renewed
connection with the Continent. The Church is re-

organised and governed by foreigners, in accordance
with the ideas that they brought with them from the
Continent.

On the other hand, William acted as the master of
the Church in England, and took careful measures to
interpose a barrier in order to prevent the intrusion of
papal authority. To say that he brought it into line
with the Church, and then that he kept it as a Church
apart, seems at first sight a manifest contradiction in
terms. Yet when we regard the general history of the
Church, we can see that there is no contradiction or
even inconsistency in his attitude. It is only, as I
insisted at the beginning, by commencing with the
history of the Church as a whole, that we can view in
its true perspective the history of that part of the
Church which was in England.

The eleventh century is, in Church history, the
great century of reform, and it divides into two quite
distinct halves. Before 1046, when the Papacy was
still unreformed, the Church as a whole had no leader,
and only a nominal head. The papal primacy was,
indeed, generally acknowledged, though the scandals
of the papal court had ruined its prestige and dis-
credited its authority. The Roman Church was still
the one from which authority was derived, and it had
long been customary for archbishops to apply to the
Pope for their pallia, and many monasteries based their
privileges on papal charters; it had long been looked
to as an authority to give a ruling on difficult questions
of law, or as an arbitrator in important disputes. But
when it departed from this passive rôle to take the

initiative, when it tried to exert its authority over an archbishop or a bishop, it was strongly and successfully resisted, and it had no means of enforcing its orders. Its position was not unlike that of the king of France, whose overlordship was recognised, though the great vassals usually disregarded his authority and only recognised it when it was of advantage to themselves, as for instance when they wished for the settlement of a legal dispute with one of their peers. The analogy is useful, because William I was one of these vassals of the king of France.

The Reform Movement, then, in the first half of the century was quite independent of the Pope and was under no single direction. It therefore took many forms. Cluny had concentrated on monastic reform; in Lorraine, where they had learnt much from Cluny, they went further and were interested in the secular clergy also. But it was principally the archbishops, the bishops, and in some cases the lay rulers, who directed the new movement. The reformers concentrated on the two principal evils of simony and clerical marriage, and on some of the abuses that resulted from lay patronage, especially over the smaller benefices, such as the holding of tithes by the laity. And naturally they tended to magnify the episcopal office and its importance, while at the same time they do not seem to have attempted to interfere with royal authority in the Church. There was certainly no objection raised to the part played by certain kings, such as Henry II and Henry III of Germany; on the contrary, it seemed as natural as it had been in the days of Charlemagne. The cause of reform was especially furthered when the kings were favourable; in fact, only when they were favourable could it make any real progress.

Among the lay rulers who played a part in this work were the dukes of Normandy. They had been in close touch especially with the reformers in Lorraine, which was later to provide bishops for England also, and they had zealously promoted reform in their duchy. A feature here as elsewhere was the foundation of monasteries; the monastic life had always been the ideal, and especially when the laxity of the secular clergy was so difficult to overcome. At the same time the dukes maintained an unchallenged authority over the Church in their duchy. Duke William acted as his predecessors had done. He was equally zealous, and quite sincerely so, as a reformer, and he was more definitely the master of the Church in his duchy. Not only, as Mr Corbett says,[1] did he "nominate all the Norman bishops and invest them with their privileges, but he was regularly present at the meetings of Church councils and no ecclesiastical decrees were issued without his sanction". He was withal zealous for good order and good government in the Church. He did not abuse his authority, like his son Rufus, and above all his appointments were usually made in the spiritual interests of the Church. His standpoint was exactly the same as that of Henry II and Henry III of Germany, and there is no doubt that it was quite in keeping with the ideas of the reformers as a whole during the first half of the eleventh century. It was in this spirit that he took in hand the management and the reform of the English Church after the Conquest of 1066.

[1] *Cambridge Medieval History*, vol. v, p. 496.

But already, twenty years before that date, reform had reached the Roman Church. By reforming the Papacy, and by nominating as Popes a series of German bishops all zealous for reform, Henry III restored to the Papacy its prestige and gave to the reform movement its natural leader. It was particularly the work of Leo IX that ensured that this should be permanent. Surrounding himself with cardinals of the same mind as himself, drawn especially from Lorraine, he made certain of the continuity of policy in the Roman Church; and by his progress north of the Alps, in France and Germany, as well as in Italy, he gave a reality to papal authority which had long been lacking, and attracted popular enthusiasm to his banner. From this time a new spirit enters into the Church. There is soon seen to be a cleavage in the ranks of the reformers. The old movement goes on, but the new movement under papal headship, in which the Church by itself sets its house in order, begins to get the upper hand and to supersede the old. The laity are still encouraged, and strongly encouraged, to help; but they are to be assistants and not directors. Moreover, as many of them do not assist, but even actively oppose reform, the movement tends to concentrate against that lay control of the Church which is often the chief bar to the success of the reformers. With Henry III and with William I cordial relations could still be maintained, but in view of the continual prevalence of simony elsewhere (and simony implies the participation of laymen) the more ardent reformers were clamouring for the removal of lay patronage and lay control of the Church.

This takes some time before it comes to the front.
Coincidently, and consequently, was gradually being
created the centralisation of the Church under papal
headship. The death of Henry III in 1056 removed
the chief bar to papal independence, which was given
a legal basis in the Election Decree of 1059. The
inability of the imperial court to interfere allowed the
process to continue unchecked, until with the accession of Gregory VII in 1073 it gathered momentum,
and in spite of deadly contest with the ruler of the
Empire eventually reached its appointed end. The
early stages of the process are all dictated by the
desire to effect the reform of the Church, which still
remains the first object even with Pope Gregory VII.
The enforcement of obedience on archbishops and
bishops, who must be responsible for executing locally
the decrees passed at Rome, is an important stage. To
ensure this obedience, the Pope gives to the legates
who are sent with his orders the power to act with full
authority in his name. Not only must the archbishop
obtain his pallium from Rome; he must go himself to
Rome to receive it, and visits to Rome are frequently
enjoined on the bishops of all countries. The Popes
directly interfere, too, in the affairs of the local
churches, great and small. It is a monarchical authority that replaces the former almost feudal headship of
the Church. The papal authority becomes a reality,
and finds expression in several directions—legal and
judicial as well as administrative. The Pope is supreme
legislator, not merely an authority on doubtful points,
and his decrees are binding on the whole Church. He
is supreme judge, to whom not only the greater cases

have to be referred. His court is a court of first instance, to which he can summon any offender. It is also a court of appeal, not only for bishops but for any of the clergy; and it is something more than a final court of appeal, for anyone can appeal at any stage, and appeal to Rome interrupts at once the proceedings in a court of first instance. Finally, the Pope is the representative of St Peter with supreme power over the souls of all men, the judge on all moral issues, the interpreter of God's will to man.

Though this is well known, it was necessary to give this brief summary in order to mark the contrast with the old position. While Reform is still the chief object, and papal centralisation only the means, there will be little quarrel with the rulers who direct the cause of reform in their kingdoms. But soon the establishment of the papal authority becomes the chief end, and while reform is still ardently pursued, it is pursued because it is a necessary part of the work to be done by the head of the Church; this makes a considerable difference in papal relations with the lay powers. The English Church starts in 1066 with the view of its master, King William I; it has come by 1215 to the view of its new master, Pope Innocent III.

This novel assertion of papal authority was not likely to pass unchallenged. In the first place, it was naturally resented by the secular authorities. It threatened to undermine the control they exercised over the episcopate, to turn their officials into papal officials, to divert from them the loyalty of some of the greatest land-holders in the country, and finally to introduce a jurisdiction that would run counter to

their own. It mattered little whether the ruler himself was in sympathy with reform or not; all were
equally affected. But it was not only the secular rulers
who disliked the new state of affairs; the bishops, and
especially the archbishops, were for the most part
thoroughly hostile to it. Their own ecclesiastical importance and authority were diminished by the authority of a dominant Pope. In many ways this became
evident.[1] The control and judgment of elections began
to pass from the metropolitans to the Pope; bishops
obtained confirmation of their elections and sometimes also consecration from the Pope. Still more did
they rebel at having to sit at their own provincial
council under the presidency of a Roman priest or
deacon, who had come as papal legate to instruct them
in the ecclesiastical affairs of their provinces or dioceses. And, again, they had to allow the authority of
their ecclesiastical courts to be flouted by any clerk
who chose to appeal to the spiritual Caesar. They did
not yield without a struggle. Siegfried, archbishop of
Mainz, who held the greatest ecclesiastical office in
Germany, was not equal to his high position but even
he could not remain silent; we can still read his rather
shrill protest against what he calls the uncanonical
action of Pope Alexander II.[2] We have also a letter of
a much more strong-minded prelate, archbishop Lie-
mar of Bremen, to a fellow bishop, in which he writes
in a tone of real indignation of the peremptory language in which the papal legates had ordered him to

---

[1] Cf. Imbart de la Tour, P., *Les élections épiscopales dans l'église
de France du ixe au xiie siècle*, pp. 476 foll. (Paris, 1891.)
[2] *Monumenta Bambergensia*, ed. Jaffé, P., pp. 85 foll.

hold a synod;[1] and he was one who had zealously promoted reform in his province. These are two examples out of many from Germany; they can be matched elsewhere. The bishops of North Italy and of France were equally hostile. The Pope had usually one answer to these outbursts—and his tone, though sometimes stern, was usually steady and composed; he had the confidence of right on his side. It was to the decrees of the Fathers, to canonical tradition—in a word, to the law of the Church—that he continually referred them. Clearly there was a conflict as to the law and its interpretation, and it soon becomes evident that it was on the law of the Church that the whole issue was to depend.

[1] Sudendorf, H., *Registrum*, 1, 5.

CHAPTER III

THE LAW OF THE WESTERN CHURCH

IT was obviously essential for this new movement of papal centralisation that it should rest on a solid basis of law, not new law, which would be suspect and resisted, but old law coming from authority that could not be gainsaid. The attitude of the Popes was quite sincere. As Gregory VII again and again repeated, they were not attempting to introduce something that was new; they wished to reveal what to them was implicit in the old decretals. The putting together of the old law of the Church so as to make it a solid foundation for the papal central government is a most interesting feature of the movement. That it is possible to trace it is due to the brilliant work of M. Paul Fournier, and anything that I can say, or that anybody can say, on this subject must be largely based on his exhaustive and very illuminating researches.

In the first place, of what did the law of the Church consist? There was no single code of law. There were a vast number of canons of Councils and decrees of Popes, genuine and false (though, of course, all were believed to be equally genuine), from which numerous collections had been made by individuals. There was not even agreement as to which councils were universally binding, and the independence of local churches is marked by the importance of decrees of their own provincial councils in the law that governed them. Also, even among the generally recognised authorities, there was considerable divergence of opinion on cer-

tain points. There had been earlier authoritative collections, which still survived. There was the collection
of Dionysius Exiguus in the fifth century, consisting
of canons of the early Councils and of decrees of
Popes, which in an expanded form was sent by Adrian I
to Charlemagne for the use of the Frankish Church—
now known as the *Dionysio-Hadriana*. There was the
collection attributed to bishop Isidore of Seville,
containing canons of Councils, Greek, African, Gallican, Spanish, followed by decrees of Popes from
about A.D. 380 onwards—now known as the *Hispana*.
Thirdly, there was the ninth-century collection with
the same attribution, the famous pseudo-Isidorian
or False Decretals, in which the forger took the
genuine *Hispana*, added in front of it a long series of
forged decrees of all the Popes prior to the Council of
Nicaea, and also inserted a number of forged decrees
into the genuine series that followed the Councils.
All of these were known indiscriminately as *Liber
Canonum*, *Corpus Canonum*, *Decreta Pontificum*, and
the like. No one collection can be said to be more
authoritative than any other; whichever happened to
be at hand to a writer in monastic or cathedral library
would be quoted. But of them the *Dionysio-Hadriana*
seems to have been much the most widely spread at
the beginning of the eleventh century; manuscripts of
tha False Decretals, on which so much was to depend
later in the century, seem to have been comparatively
scarce at the beginning. These collections, however,
all had a serious defect from the standpoint of the
person who wanted to consult them. They were
arranged in a purely chronological order, not accord-

ing to subject, so that the use of them was a difficult and a lengthy business.

There had been previous collections arranged in a systematic way according to subject-matter, for instance that of Regino of Prum. But now early in the eleventh century (just about the time that Lanfranc was born) appeared the great work of bishop Burchard of Worms, arranged in twenty books, the *Decretum* or *Collectarium*. This became the popular work, widely used for half a century, and continuing to be employed occasionally even in the twelfth century. It is therefore the normal text-book of Church law during the earlier period of reform. And it fitted very well with the ideas of the time. Burchard is quite clear as to the divine institution of the Papacy and its headship of the Church. It is the source of law, for, as M. Fournier points out, he employs papal decretals as his chief authority, while he even goes to the length of ascribing to Popes documents which certainly did not emanate from them, including extracts from the civil law; and he admits the rule that conciliar decrees are only valid if they have received papal recognition. It is also the source of authority. All metropolitans have to send to the Pope their professions of faith and to ask for the pallium within three months of consecration; the Pope, too, has authority to prevent vacancies in sees and to intervene in translations; all major or difficult cases should be brought to Rome, and bishops have always the right of appeal to Rome. "The apostolic see is the hinge on which the whole Church turns".[1]

---

[1] Fournier, P., *Le Décret de Burchard de Worms* (Revue d'histoire ecclésiastique, vol. XII, 1911, pp. 468 foll.).

But it is evident how much this falls short of the later view; there is little in it that indicates any idea of the Papacy directly governing the Church. Very few chapters in this large collection mention the Papacy at all; the references to it are most exiguous. This is entirely in keeping with the general attitude towards the Papacy which I have already described. What Burchard does stress at great length is the importance of the bishop and of episcopal authority; it may be noted that monastic exemptions are not mentioned by him at all. He regards the bishops, says M. Fournier,[1] as "the ordinary and normal organ of spiritual government, under the distant control of the Pope, which control is exercised rarely and only in grave cases, but under the immediate control of assemblies of bishops of the province". It is noticeable how many decrees of local councils in France and Germany in the ninth and tenth centuries he includes in his *Decretum*. He stresses very strongly the two great evils attacked by the early reformers— simony and clerical marriage—and even considerably widens the definition of simony. To the interference of the lay ruler he is certainly opposed, though he allows him some part in ecclesiastical affairs; in practice he worked in great harmony with the Emperor Henry II. On the whole, the *Decretum* of Burchard may be said to be exactly in the mood of the time: it was urgent for reform, but left the direction of it to the bishop or the provincial synod; the Pope was the source of authority and of law, but not an active

---

[1] *Ib.* p. 473.

master; he was the final arbiter to whom the most difficult matters should be referred.

It is evident at first sight that this would not be regarded as a satisfactory manual of Church law by the partisans of a strong central government of the Church. What they needed was a collection in which the whole law of the Church would radiate from the Papacy, and would make everything dependent on the supreme will of the Head of the Church. Not the bishop and the provincial council but the Pope and the Roman Church must be the normal organ of government, the bishops his subordinates to obey his orders, his court the supreme court to which any of the clergy might appeal, and under whose protection monasteries and even princes might place themselves. Also it must be uniform. It was Roman Church law that was required for the papal government of the Church, and in this must be included only the decrees of Popes and of such Councils as the Popes considered authoritative. But on the whole the need was not so much to check the authorities used as to make a different selection from the universally recognised authorities. The pseudo-Isidorian Decretals were a thoroughly satisfactory quarry by themselves; from them alone could be extracted a manual expressing all that the Papacy wished to be expressed. Burchard had used them as one of his chief sources, both at first and second hand; but he was careful to select only such passages as agreed with his ideas of Church government. What was required was for someone to approach them with a new purpose, and to use them

more truly in the way in which their original compiler
had meant them to be used.

A beginning was made already in Leo IX's Papacy
with the appearance about 1050 of an anonymous
Collection in 74 Titles.[1] It is a mere fragment compared with the large work of Burchard, but when the
comparison is made of what each has to say about the
power and authority of the Papacy, Burchard appears
fragmentary beside it. The authority of the Papacy and
the reform programme are its two themes. And it
derives almost entirely from two sources—the False
Decretals and the writings of Gregory the Great—the
two authorities, by the way, on which Gregory VII
himself almost entirely depended. It is not a manual
of Church law, but only as it were a preface to such a
manual. What it did, however, it did well. It left its
mark on all future collections; no later collection did
in fact ignore the basic principles that it laid down.
And it obtained a wide currency; especially in an expanded form, and with an addition in the form of a
number of extracts from Councils, it travelled as far
west as Spain and as far north as England.

Three other collections, dating from the pontificate
of Gregory VII, have been described by M. Fournier[2]
—those of Cardinal Atto, bishop Anselm of Lucca,
and Cardinal Deusdedit. Cardinals Atto and Deusdedit were similarly limited in scope, though with

[1] Fournier, P., *Le premier manuel canonique de la réforme du xi*[e]
siècle (École française de Rome. Mélanges d'archéologie et d'histoire,
vol. XIV, pp. 147–223. Rome, 1894).
[2] *Les collections canoniques romaines de l'époque de Grégoire VII*
(Mémoires de l'Institut National de France. Académie des Inscrip-
tions et Belles Lettres, vol. XLI, pp. 271–397. Paris, 1920).

greater wealth of material. And again the character of their collections unfitted them for use as legal manuals. Atto's *Capitulare* was a chronological compilation, concentrating on the Roman Church and the reform programme—a source-book and nothing more. Deusdedit was wider in his range; he drew into his net much new material from the decrees of recent reforming Popes. But he confined himself to the Roman Church, dealing in four books with its primacy, its clergy, its property, and its privileges. Within each book, though he divided his authorities into categories, he retained otherwise the chronological method. It was a more complete source-book than Atto's, but not much more use to the canonical practician. Bishop Anselm's collection was of a different order. It was in thirteen books and was arranged according to subject-matter, so that it was a systematic collection. It derived from former collections, both chronological and systematic; it used both Burchard and the *Collection in 74 Titles* as well as the False Decretals, and, like Deusdedit, Anselm included much new material. He discarded practically all the later provincial councils used by Burchard, everything in fact which he judged not to be Roman or conformable to the Roman tradition. His book was much the most complete of the new collections, for he was concerned with all sides of ecclesiastical legislation; but like the others he put papal authority and the reform programme into the forefront. His work was much used by pro-papal controversialists, and, unlike those of Atto and Deusdedit, which seem to have been only locally important, it reached countries

outside Italy. As a result of these collections the new
position was established, and the *Decretum* of Burchard, useful still as a source-book though only one
among many, had an antiquated outlook and was out-
of-date. No collection now could ignore the numerous
texts that emphasised papal authority in all directions,
or could fail to stress it as the central and directing
force in the government and legislation of the whole
Church.

The collection of bishop Anselm of Lucca is described by M. Fournier as the first of a chain of
canonical collections mainly Italian, which culminate
in Gratian. The further stages of advance are marked
by the new scientific study both of civil and canon
law, for which Bologna was already famous in the
latter part of the eleventh century. In this there are
two main points. Firstly, textual accuracy, or at
least honesty. In the earlier collections, especially in
Burchard and Deusdedit, there was a considerable
amount of slight alteration to make the text suit more
exactly the author's point of view, or of wrong ascrip-
tion of authorities, which in Burchard's case was
certainly deliberate. Many of his wrong ascriptions
have been copied from him by later collections, but
in their case quite innocently. Secondly, in jurisprudence. No longer do the canonists merely seek for
material that accords with their views; they are
anxious to use all the authorities and to harmonise or
explain or decide between conflicting statements. The
work was done systematically. They were not content
merely to utilise older collections, such as Burchard or
the *Collection in 74 Titles*, and add additional matter

to them. They went back to the originals and made
their own abstracts, to which they added numerous
extracts from later collections as well, before arrang-
ing the whole in order according to subject-matter.
English manuscripts in particular provide more than
one example of this; it is noticeable that an abstract of
pseudo-Isidore, both decretals and Councils, forms
the first and the chief part of these preliminary
collections, while a second regular ingredient is an
abstract of the letters of Gregory the Great. Usually
this preliminary collection of material was doubtless
destroyed after it had served its purpose and had been
re-arranged into its final form. There is one such
collection, however, which has survived in a number
of copies—the *Tripartita* or *Collectio trium partium*.
The great importance of this collection, which has
been fully described by M. Fournier,[1] lies in the
fact that it was used by Ivo of Chartres as the basis
of his later systematic collections,[2] and perhaps
it was actually, as M. Fournier thinks, compiled
by him.

From this and similar collections of abstracts, with
the aid too of the earlier collections that have been
mentioned, it was possible to advance to the next
stage, and to compile a comprehensive work of Church
law arranged according to subject-matter. This, in
particular, was the achievement of Ivo of Chartres at

---

[1] *Les collections canoniques attribuées à Yves de Chartres* (Bibl. de
l'école des chartres, vol. LVII, pp. 645–698. Paris, 1896). Cf. also,
Wasserschleben, H., *Beiträge zur Geschichte der vorgratian. Kirchenrechtsquellen* (Leipzig, 1839).

[2] This applies to the first two parts only. The third part is clearly
an abstract of Ivo's *Decretum*.

the end of the eleventh century.[1] His *Decretum* in
seventeen parts was his first attempt in this direction;
it had little vogue, because the author himself was not
satisfied with it, but he made use of it to compile the
shorter and much more handy *Pannormia* in eight
books. This was the popular text-book in the first half
of the twelfth century, and was even more widely
used than Burchard's *Decretum* had been a century
earlier. It alone survived the appearance of Gratian's
Decretum, and in the thirteenth century a number of
copies of it were still being made. But Gratian's
Decretum in the second half of the twelfth century did
in fact supersede it as well as all other collections. This
marks the final stage in the codification of the old law,
and there is now one collection universally recognised and annotated. It was the authoritative collection, too; for the later collections, the *Decretales* of
Gregory IX and its successors, are concerned with
new law and are definitely supplementary to Gratian;
and it therefore forms the first part of the *Corpus
Juris Canonici* of the Roman Church.

I have gone into these details, many of which I
have perforce had to take second-hand from M.
Fournier, in order to depict the change in the character
of Church law that took place during the century and
a half from Burchard to Gratian. The difference
between them is enormous in outlook: as the centralisation of the Church under papal government has
become the prime feature of Church history, so this is
mirrored in the law by which the Church is governed;

---

[1] Cf. Fournier, P., *op. cit.* vols. LVII and LVIII, and his summary
in vol. LVIII, p. 675.

---

uniformity to Roman practice has become the rule; the reform programme, common to them both, is now directed by the Pope and is subject to a mass of new papal legislation. The change naturally does not receive universal acceptance at once. Where, as in France, papal authority becomes quickly established, the law as recognised in Rome is there recognised as well. On the other hand, the new collections provided one of the chief means by which the Papacy was able to extend its authority. When archbishop Siegfried in 1074 wrote to Gregory VII, complaining of the uncanonical action of his predecessor Alexander II in punishing a bishop of the province of Mainz whose case had not first been brought before the metropolitan and heard by the bishops of his province, he was maintaining a standpoint which Burchard would have championed. "Uncanonical!" says Gregory in his reply. "My brother, we invite you to peruse with us the canonical traditions and the decrees of the holy fathers".[1] Doubtless he had particularly in mind a passage from a letter of Pope Gelasius I.[2] He possibly read it in the *Collection in 74 Titles*, which had extracted it from the False Decretals; henceforward it is one of the regular entries in canonical collections, and finally is incorporated in Gratian's *Decretum*.[3] And just as archbishop Siegfried was crushed and made no further attempt to quote canonical authority against the Pope, so it was with others. At first the acquiescence is sullen and enforced. But this changes later, especially in France and North Italy, to a willing

[1] Reg. 1.60, ed. Caspar, E. (M.G.H., *Epistolae selectae*, II, 1), p. 88.
[2] *Ib.* p. 88, n. 1.   [3] C. IX, qu. 3, c. 17.

obedience. And I think that part of the explanation,
the chief part, lies in the new canonical collections in
which the rising generation was being trained. The
young students of Church law read that the first duty
was obedience to the Pope; the first place was given
to papal authority throughout. And the final stage was
reached when the multiplicity of collections, mirroring
the different views of individuals, yielded to one single
collection, universally recognised and mirroring the
papal view. It took a hundred years to reach this final
development. Acceptance came at an early stage in
France. What happened there was to happen, though
somewhat later, in England also. It is this fact that I
hope to establish in the pages that immediately follow,
and to show the same change taking place, in exactly
the same way, in the English Church as in the Western
Church as a whole.

PART I

THE LAW OF THE CHURCH IN ENGLAND

CHAPTER IV

THE METHOD OF THIS ENQUIRY

IN what I have said already about the Western Church as a whole, I have tried to make it clear that, while there was no difference of opinion as to the unity of the Church and the papal headship of the Church, there was considerable doubt as to the meaning to be attached to headship, as to the extent of papal authority, and therefore as to the details of ecclesiastical law. The English Church after the Conquest was controlled by men who came from, and brought their ideas from, the Continent; it was not in these respects distinct from the other Churches in Europe. Previous to the Conquest, it had, in its isolation, been tending to develop certain distinctive characteristics; the chief peculiarities that survived the Conquest were the monastic control of certain cathedrals and the payment of Peter's Pence, but there was nothing which gave a particularly English flavour to ecclesiastical administration and legislation. The features which do tend to differentiate it from other Churches are almost entirely of post-Conquest growth, and mainly of a political rather than an ecclesiastical nature; at any rate their origin must be sought rather on the Continent than in England.

This is not surprising when we consider the condition of the English Church at the time of the Conquest. The bishops were mostly uneducated and secularised, the lower clergy hopelessly ignorant; ecclesiastical synods and ecclesiastical law had fallen into disuse, and there was no separate ecclesiastical jurisdiction. Moreover, the reform movement played no part in England, where simony, clerical marriage, and other abuses attacked by the reformers went on as a matter of course. The Church needed to be purified and reorganised from top to bottom. The reform programme was introduced; the episcopate was purged; ecclesiastical courts were created; ecclesiastical synods were revived; and an entirely new personnel, brought in from the Continent, was given charge of the ecclesiastical administration. But, for the working of this new organisation, there had to be a complete body of laws and regulations. The decrees passed at synods covered only a limited number of points. What, then, was the general law by which the English Church was governed and administered, and which directed the procedure of its courts?

There was, indeed, a good deal that might have been culled from the past, if the memory of it had survived. There had been considerable legislation for the English Church at different times. And, moreover, the British Isles had made their own contribution to the general law of the Church. There were, first of all, the Penitentials, all of them in origin Irish or English, a system which made the punishment fit the crime in a manner familiar in the secular laws of the Teutonic peoples; they had become very popular on the Continent, and Burchard of Worms made considerable use of them, though the Roman Church was beginning in the second half of the century to frown upon them. They survived, indeed, in England and continued to play a part, but only a very subordinate one; and, it must be remembered, they were often written in Anglo-Saxon, which was unintelligible to the new rulers of the Church.[1] There was, secondly, the Irish canonical collection of the eighth century,[2] a systematic collection, which had played a great part in the reform of the Frankish Church, and which had become important again in Italy in the early eleventh century. Burchard of Worms made considerable use of it, and indeed he had much in common with it, both in his attitude to reform and to the part played by the Pope; Ivo of Chartres and Gratian culled extracts from it second-hand from Burchard. Its particular contribution to Church law consisted in its extracts from the Bible and the Fathers; previously decrees of Popes and canons of Councils had been almost exclusively used as the authorities. There are a few English manuscripts of it, one of which seems to have been in the possession of archbishop Dunstan. But there is no evidence at all that this general collection or the particular legislation of the Anglo-Saxon Church were used and studied, or even known, after the Conquest. And when we come to Norman collections of law, such as the *Leges Henrici primi*, we find that the ecclesiastical law contained in them, unlike the secular law, is derived entirely from sources that had come into England after the Conquest—mainly from Ivo of Chartres, with additions from the False Decretals and their companion forgery, the *Capitula*

---

[1] Cf. Graham, Miss Rose, *English Ecclesiastical Studies*, p. 159.
[2] Fournier, P., *De l'influence de la collection irlandaise sur la formation des collections canoniques* (Nouvelle revue historique de droit français et étranger, vol. XXIII, pp. 27–78. Paris, 1899).

Ingilramni.[1] Collections, such as the *Dionysio-Hadriana*, which were known in this country at an earlier date, seem to have been no longer studied; at any rate, little trace of them remains to-day.[2]

Taking it for granted, then, that we have to look outside England for the ideas and influences which controlled the development of the post-Conquest Church, and especially of the law by which it was governed, it is vital to the enquiry on which we are engaged to discover if any, one or more, of the known collections of which I have spoken were adopted in this country. On what did the prelates, the ecclesiastical courts, the teachers and students of canon law depend? It is vital to our enquiry, because it is only if we can get an answer to that question that we can say what must have been the official attitude with regard to the new papal claims that were being put forward, and also to the relationship in which the English Church should stand to the Papacy. It is, at the same time, a difficult question to answer in a definite manner, because, as we have seen, there were so many different views in the Church as a whole as to what the law of the Church really was. It is not until the middle of the twelfth century, when the *Decretum* of Gratian appeared, that there was general agreement even upon the Continent. I need not say that,

[1] Liebermann, F., *Ueber das Englische Rechtsbuch Leges Henrici* (Halle, 1901). Pollock and Maitland, *History of English Law,* vol. 1, 2nd ed. pp. 99 foll., wrongly designate Burchard as the source from which the author extracted his ecclesiastical regulations.

[2] There is a Bodleian MS. (Hatton 42), which contains the "Irish" collection and part of the *Dionysio-Hadriana* (the Greek Councils only). This MS. was apparently brought to Glastonbury in the tenth century.

as far as England is concerned, this is a question which
has been hotly debated and has become highly con-
troversial. But most of the controversy has been
built upon speculation and hypothesis; so far no one
has really made an investigation to discover what were
the actual collections that were available before the
introduction of Gratian.

It is advisable to begin by reviewing the various
possible sources of evidence. If we want to know
what collections were used at any particular time, we
must first try to discover what were available for use.
First of all, we may hope to learn this from the
medieval catalogues of libraries, cathedral and monastic, that survive. But there are not many of them;
none of them date back to the eleventh century, and
only a very few to the twelfth century, though occasionally some further indication is given by a record
of the gifts of an early donor, such as Lanfranc to
Christ Church, Canterbury. Again, those that do survive are often incomplete; for instance, in the twelfth-
century catalogue of Christ Church the canon law
section is missing. Moreover, even if we possessed
complete catalogues of all the libraries that were then
in existence, we should still be considerably in the
dark. For though these catalogues give precise information with regard to biblical commentaries, the
early Fathers, classical writers, and the like, about
canon law they are much less particular, at any rate
about the pre-Gratian material. The description of
volumes as *Decreta Pontificum*, *Canones*, *Corpus Canonum*, and the like, tell us nothing certain. They are

all equally applicable to any collection of decrees and canons, as can be proved by existing manuscripts which bear these headings. The only thing we can say is that almost certainly, to judge again from existing manuscripts, the description does denote one of the known collections and not just a chance collection made by some individual scribe. But it makes all the difference to our investigation whether the collection was, for instance, the genuine *Hispana* or the forged Isidore or, it may be, one of the collections made at Rome in the second half of the eleventh century, or even the *Tripartita* attributed to Ivo of Chartres. The only exception to this is in the case of the two collections which were certainly compiled by Ivo of Chartres; these are usually both described as *Decreta Yvonis*, though in almost every case it must be his *Pannormia* and not his *Decretum* that is meant.[1] Medieval catalogues, then, provide us with a very limited amount of information, and this would in fact be almost useless to us without the assistance of existing manuscripts.

Another source of evidence lies in the writings of contemporaries, who, especially when engaged in a controversy like that which raged around Becket, do sometimes quote from ecclesiastical law, especially from papal decrees and canons of Councils. But, naturally, they are only concerned with giving the authorities in favour of their view, and they never in-

---

[1] There is a further complication arising from the inaccuracy of some of these catalogues. Thus a manuscript of Burchard's *Decretum* in the cathedral library of Durham (B. IV, 17) is described, both on the manuscript itself and in the medieval catalogues, as *Decreta Yvonis*.

form us of the book from which they extracted the quotations. Occasionally, however, it is possible to discover which was the actual collection that they were using; in the case of Lanfranc this can, by the aid of existing manuscripts, be stated with practical certainty, and there is nobody about whom it is more valuable to possess this knowledge. Moreover, even when the collection from which the quotations are made is not known, the quotations themselves often indicate the attitude of the writer to the question of papal authority, and are therefore very relevant to my main line of enquiry.

With these two sources, library catalogues and contemporary writers, I shall deal later on in their proper place. For they are, in a sense, subordinate and supplementary to my third source of information. By themselves what they tell us is very meagre; but wc can learn considerably more from them when we utilise the much more precise information which can be derived from existing manuscripts. It is on these that we have primarily to rely, and this source has to be minutely explored. So my first objective is to discover what manuscripts there are now existing which contain collections of ecclesiastical law, and which one can reasonably assume to have been in England in the eleventh and twelfth centuries. From them we can obtain a very considerable amount of perfectly definite evidence.

Of course, the tale of what is now in existence presents only a fraction of the truth, since vast numbers of manuscripts have perished leaving no trace behind them. And one feels that the hand of destruction must especially have lain heavily upon collections of law that were constantly invoking papal authority, when one reads the commission given by Henry VIII to Leland (which that eminent antiquarian was not always scrupulous to obey) or the Privy Council minute of 25 February 1551: "for the purging of his Highnes librarie at Westminster of all superstitious bookes".[1] Further, it is with the old law books that we are concerned, which became out-of-date on the appearance of Gratian's *Decretum*; and doubtless many of them had already suffered the fate which Leland in the sixteenth century describes, when speaking of St Augustine's, Canterbury: "the ignorant monks tore up the Greek books, which they did not understand, and the Latin ones, which were too old to please them, and employed them to line the book shelves, to mention no meaner uses".[2]

Then, again, the technical difficulties of such an enquiry are extremely formidable. It is no easy question to decide whether a manuscript, written in or before the twelfth century, was actually in this country at that time. In default of other evidence, one has to depend on the handwriting. I cannot pretend to be more than an amateur in palaeography, but I have had the advantage of getting expert opinion, at Cambridge and Oxford, at the British Museum and Eton, which makes me feel much more confident about my answers to these particular difficulties. Naturally, too, I have

[1] Cf. Introduction to the *Catalogue of the Royal and Kings' MSS. in the British Museum*.

[2] Cf. James, M. R., *Ancient Libraries of Canterbury and Dover*, pp. lxxix foll.

gained considerable assistance on these points from the modern catalogues of manuscripts. But they are much less helpful in identifying collections of ecclesiastical law; and there are many collections of manuscripts, such as the great Cottonian collection in the British Museum, which still await a modern cataloguer. The indices of catalogues, whether recent or not, have been practically valueless for my purpose. So it has been necessary, first of all, to read through the catalogues of all English libraries that contain manuscripts, noting everything that seemed to be relevant to my subject; and, secondly, to investigate a large number of manuscripts in all parts of the country. The task is a vast one, and I do not pretend that I have been able to complete it. Nor have I attempted the still harder task of trying to discover the English manuscripts which have migrated to the Continent since the twelfth century; possibly the catalogue now being made of the Vatican manuscripts may bring some of these to light.

And yet, though many of the manuscripts are irretrievably lost, and though my search among the surviving ones is not completed, it has already proved to be far more fruitful than I had anticipated. From it one can trace the development of canon law in England, almost with precision as far as the second half of the eleventh century is concerned; in less distinct outline, though with more material, in the first half of the twelfth century; and perfectly clearly again in the second half of the twelfth century, and onwards. Above all, the material that I have collected enables me to arrive at certain quite definite conclusions as to the law by which the English Church was governed, and therefore the official attitude to papal authority. So confident am I in these conclusions that I am prepared to burn my boats and to predict that, whatever additions and corrections may be made to my material, the conclusions I have drawn from it will remain unaltered.

CHAPTER V

LANFRANC'S COLLECTION

OBVIOUSLY it is with Lanfranc that we must start this enquiry, for the character of the organisation and legislation of the newly reformed Church in England depended upon his judgment. In saying this, I am not leaving out of account the part played by the Conqueror, which will be dealt with later. William acted as master of the Church, but the details of its government were left in the hands of Lanfranc. I am considering, from the ecclesiastical standpoint, the law which was accepted, which was the object of study, and which informed the rising generation; this was Lanfranc's province, and his was clearly the directing and controlling mind.

The law of the Church was a question, too, in which he was bound to be profoundly interested. His early training in Italy had been in the civil law, of which he had also been a teacher. It was probably not until he went to Bec that he took up the study of theology, and he may have started his study of canon law there as well. When he became archbishop, the importance of the law must have presented itself at once to his legal mind, and we can hardly be wrong in imagining that he would refer at once to the library at Bec for the collection, or collections, which he had read and studied there. Of the library at Bec there is in existence a twelfth-century, probably early twelfth-century, catalogue,[1]

---

[1] Ravaisson, F., *Rapports sur les bibliothèques des départements de l'Ouest*, Appendix 13, pp. 375 foll. (Paris, 1841.)

which contains the names of some half a dozen volumes dealing with ecclesiastical law. Four of them bear the vague titles I mentioned above—*Decreta Pontificum, Canones, Excerpta Decretorum, Corpus Canonum*; a fifth is a pontifical after the Roman order. The sixth has a definite name: the *Collectiones* (i.e. *Decretum*) of Burchard in twenty books, and the enthusiastic cataloguer goes on to describe it as "necessary for the conduct of ecclesiastical and secular affairs alike". It would be very interesting to know whether Lanfranc studied this at Bec. It is tempting to believe that he did, for his general standpoint in ecclesiastical affairs is in so many respects similar to that of Burchard. But, though it may possibly have helped to form his point of view, there is no evidence that he actually used a copy in his work as archbishop in England, or that there was any copy of Burchard in England at that time. So the library at Bec affords us little real help. When we follow Lanfranc from Bec to Canterbury we do not get any farther. The twelfth-century catalogue of Christ Church, Canterbury[1] is only a fragment, and the section on canon law is unfortunately missing. From a later catalogue we learn that he was the donor of five volumes—a book of homilies, a Priscian, and three copies of the Pauline Epistles. This is of no use for our purpose.

We make more progress when we try another line, and look for references in his writings. In a letter to bishop Herfast of Thetford,[2] he adjures him to give

---

[1] James, M. R., *The Ancient Libraries of Canterbury and Dover*, pp. 7-12.
[2] *Epp.*, ed. Giles, J. A., no. 26.

up dice and secular games and to read the Scriptures, and especially to study the decrees of the Roman pontiffs and the sacred canons; he goes on to quote decrees and canons bearing on the position of the metropolitan. In other letters, too, he quotes from, or refers his correspondent to, the " canons and decrees of the holy fathers". Besides his letters, there is another important source—the decrees of his first council, the Council of London in 1075, which were carefully drawn up and widely disseminated. It opens with a statement that "some things were revived anew, which had been laid down in ancient canons"; and the nine canons of this Council are based on ancient authority, which in some cases is actually quoted, and is taken, with the one exception of the Rule of St Benedict, from canons of Councils and from papal decrees (in no case later than Gregory II). From all this we see that he was relying on some collection containing mainly, if not entirely, papal decrees and canons of Councils. It was not Burchard, because, though some of his quotations are to be found in Burchard, there are more that are not in Burchard at all. Can we discover which was the collection that he was using? and, secondly, what is equally import-ant, whether there is any evidence that other people used it as well?

Both these questions can, I believe, be answered in the affirmative, and to the first of them the answer is most suitably[1] to be found in a manuscript of Trinity

---

[1] Since it was in Trinity College that the lectures, on which this book is based, were delivered. The MS. in question is no. 405 (B. 16. 44).

College, Cambridge, written in the eleventh century, possibly about or shortly before 1070. It is a collection of decrees and canons, and its association with Lanfranc is undoubted. On the last folio it is stated that "I Lanfranc archbishop bought this book and had it brought from Bec and presented it to the church of Christ". These words were not, indeed, written by Lanfranc himself, but they were, I feel sure, dictated by him. And there is further evidence, to be described later, which makes definite the association with Lanfranc. From this manuscript Dr James[1] has drawn certain conclusions most important from the point of view of the student of handwriting. Certain other conclusions can be drawn from it still more important for the student of Church history. For I believe that this was the book from which Lanfranc was quoting; that it was this collection of papal decrees and canons of Councils which he used as his authority; and that copies of it were widely distributed, so that it became the basis of the study of ecclesiastical law in England.

Now as to its contents. It is, in fact, a copy of the False Decretals, but it is not a complete copy and in certain other respects it bears a marked individuality of its own. The normal pseudo-Isidore is in three parts: the papal decretals from Clement to Melchiades, the Councils from Nicaea to Seville II, the papal decretals from Sylvester I to Gregory II. This manuscript is in two parts: first, the papal decretals continuously from Clement to Gregory II with certain additions at the end; then, the Councils from

---

[1] *The Ancient Libraries of Canterbury and Dover*, p. xxx.

Nicaea to Seville II. The papal decretals are not complete, but abridged. Some letters are given in full, some are omitted altogether, from some large portions have been left out: the first three letters of Clement are given in full, the other two are omitted; prior to the fourth century, there are fewer omissions than later, but most of the letters are abridged; afterwards, the omissions are more numerous, but the letters included are usually given in full. In all, the bulk is reduced by at least one-third, possibly by almost one-half. This abridgment, however, so far as I have been able to judge from my study of the manuscript, does not alter in the least the character of the collection. The object of the person who made the abridgment seems to have been to leave out what was otiose or of little import-ance, so as to retain in a smaller compass the real pith of the collection, all the more important papal decisions. At any rate there seems to have been no disposition to exclude anything which gives the False Decretals their distinctive character; where I have checked it, I have found the important assertions of papal authority intact. So the character of the col-lection seems to have been integrally preserved; but the reduction in bulk made it much easier to use, and this was doubtless the purpose of the compiler.

The Councils, on the other hand, are given in full, but here again the collection is unique. The Greek Councils are in the older, *Dionysio-Hadriana*, version (except for Ephesus, which was not in that version); Ephesus and the African, Gallican, and Spanish Councils are in the version of Isidore and follow the pseudo-Isidorian text. There are some variations of an unimportant character, but sufficiently marked to make this collection again very definitely recognisable, and to distinguish it from other copies of the False Decretals.

This difference of treatment is not in itself surprising. In the making of letters there is plenty of material which can easily be excluded by the compiler who is seeking for legal judgments only; while there is little of this otiose matter in Councils, which are strictly concerned with legislation. But, as a matter of fact, the two parts of this manuscript were quite separately compiled and derive from different originals. The first part must have been an abridgment of a manuscript (and there are a certain number of these in existence) which contained only decretals, while the second part was an exact copy of a manuscript containing the Councils. There is plenty of evidence to show that this book is really composed of two books, separately compiled, which have been put together into one volume. Not only are the two parts derived from different originals. They are written by different scribes, and the two parts were separately put together and have separate signatures on the sheets. It is quite clear that there were two distinct manuscripts, one of papal decretals, the other of Councils, which were written about the same time and were very likely bound together at an early date, possibly when they were required by Lanfranc.

Now, Lanfranc was not the only person who possessed this particular collection of the False Decretals. Hinschius, in his edition of the False Decretals,[1]

[1] Introduction, pp. lxxiii–lxxvi.

describes a group of eight manuscripts, which I find agree exactly with Lanfranc's manuscript. Three of them are in French libraries (one at Paris, two at Rouen), and contain the decretals only; another (at Paris) contains the Councils followed by the decretals; the other four are in English libraries (three at the British Museum, one in the Lincoln cathedral library), and contain both decretals and Councils. Further, H. Böhmer[1] briefly discusses Lanfranc's manuscript, and associates with it the three British Museum manuscripts mentioned by Hinschius and also two others— in the libraries of Peterhouse and Corpus Christi College, Cambridge; these also I find agree exactly and contain both decretals and Councils. Finally, I have myself discovered three more complete copies, one in Salisbury cathedral library, and two in the Hereford cathedral library (the second of which is, I believe, a copy of the first, and is in two separate volumes); while I have also found in the Bodleian a manuscript of the Councils which is a copy of the second part of this collection.

Here, then, we have a group of fifteen manuscripts[2] which present this collection in whole or in part. In the first place there is a distinction between the French and the English copies, in that the French (with the exception of the Paris manuscript mentioned above, which is of late and unknown origin) contain the

---

[1] *Die Fälschungen Erzbischof Lanfranks von Canterbury*, pp. 61–82. He is discussing three monastic forgeries, which were written in at the very end of Lanfranc's manuscript, and which he attributes (I think quite wrongly) to Lanfranc himself. I hope to deal with these in a separate article.

[2] For a fuller description of these manuscripts, see Appendix.

decretals only, while the English (with the exception of the Bodleian manuscript) have both decretals and Councils. This fact is interesting, because it indicates further proof that the decretals and Councils derive from separate originals and were only put together for English use.   But otherwise the resemblances are much more striking than the differences. The English manuscripts, with the exception of Lanfranc's copy, seem certainly to have all been written in this country. As to the French manuscripts, the two at Rouen come from the Norman abbey of Jumièges. One of the Paris manuscripts is also of Norman origin, in all probability; it is one of the Codices Bigotini presented to the Bibliothèque Nationale, most of which came from Normandy. The other Paris manuscript is exceptional in every way, as I have mentioned; its origin is unknown, but it is relatively unimportant, since it is a late copy of the fifteenth century. All the other copies belong to the late eleventh or to the twelfth, mostly early twelfth, century. So we can say that this collection was confined to Normandy and England, and that it had its vogue in the second half of the eleventh century and the first half of the twelfth. Between the French and the English manuscripts Lanfranc's copy forms the connecting link. The collection of decretals appears to be one that was only to be found in Normandy until Lanfranc brought it, together with a copy of the Councils, to England, where in this complete form it had a still greater vogue.

Time and place alike suggest an association with Lanfranc. There is another and a closer link. In the fourteen manuscripts which contain the decretals,[1] these do not end in the usual way with Gregory II. There follow, not only the *Capitula Ingilramni*, a companion forgery to pseudo-Isidore which often accompanies it in manuscripts, but also three further documents, which are a much more unusual addition —(*a*) a decretal letter of Pope Nicholas II detailing the chief decrees of the Lateran synod of 1059, (*b*) the collection of decrees against simony from the same synod,[2] (*c*) the oath of Berengar of Tours at that synod, recanting his heresy. There can only be one reason for the addition of this material, of a date three centuries later than any other documents in the collection. Clearly Lanfranc was responsible. He was present himself at the synod of 1059 on the business of William I's marriage, and the oath of Berengar was of especial interest to him; in his book against Berengar he quotes it in full and refers to it several times. In that book he also refers to Berengar's second recantation in 1079, which is added in some of the manuscripts of this collection; not indeed in Lanfranc's copy, which, for this and other reasons, I believe to have been written before 1079. But it was a natural addition to have been made in later copies.

In Lanfranc's manuscript it is stated that it was brought from Bec. My belief is that there was a

---

[1] More correctly, in thirteen out of the fourteen. One of the Rouen manuscripts is defective at the end, and therefore does not contain these additions, but doubtless it did in its original form.

[2] I feel no difficulty, as some people have, in dating these documents from the same synod. The first is an encyclical by the Pope, summarising the chief decrees of the synod, the second gives the actual text of the decrees dealing with simony.

complete copy of the Decretals at Bec, from which
this abridgment was made, and that on this complete
copy the three extra documents had previously been
written at Lanfranc's direction while he was still at
Bec. There is further confirmation of this inference.
I have said that they are an unusual addition to
manuscripts of the False Decretals. In fact, I only
know of four other manuscripts where they occur,
and these happen to be the only four manuscripts of
English origin containing the Decretals in full that I
have been able to find. I shall deal with these manuscripts more fully in the following chapter, but here I
want briefly to summarise the conclusions which I
shall then detail by saying that these four manuscripts
—two of the twelfth century, two of the fifteenth—
clearly derive from an original which contained the
Decretals and not the Councils, and that that original
included also the documents of the 1059 synod. It
must, I feel sure, have been at Bec, and also it must
have been from this same original that Lanfranc's
abridged collection was compiled.[1] In the library at

---

[1] H. Böhmer in his account of the Lanfranc MS. (see above, p. 63)
also associates with it three of these four MSS. which contain the
decretals unabridged. I may say that I only became aware that he
had associated Lanfranc with the introduction of pseudo-Isidore
into England after I had arrived at the same conclusion independently;
but I owe to him my first knowledge of the Peterhouse and Corpus
Christi MSS. He does not seem to realise the full importance of this
conclusion, which has remained unnoticed save for a brief reference
in Professor Haskins' *Norman Institutions*, p. 30. Moreover, his
treatment of the MSS. is far from satisfactory, as he confounds
complete and abridged MSS. together, associating them all with
Lanfranc. In my view the complete MSS. are really independent of
Lanfranc. They are linked up with the abridged collection owing to
a common association with Bec.

Bec, as I have said, there were, at any rate shortly after Lanfranc's time, five volumes containing collections of ecclesiastical law. One of them, *Decreta Pontificum*, might well be the original volume of complete decretals; *Excerpta Decretorum* might be a copy of part 1 of Lanfranc's book, which bears the same heading, though it might equally be a copy of a collection such as the *Tripartita*; and either *Canones* or *Corpus Canonum* would fit either a collection of Councils or a collection of both decretals and Councils.

This, however, is only hypothesis. What is much more to the purpose is the probability, I might almost say certainty, that it was this book which he used as his authority, and that his quotations from canon law were taken from it. He makes use of forged as well as of genuine decretals; therefore he must have used either the Forged Decretals or a collection which employed them. Burchard's *Decretum* will not fit the case, nor will any other collection that I know. And as he quotes decrees and canons none of which are later than Gregory II, the presumption is that he is directly quoting from the False Decretals. If so, we can reasonably infer that he used the copy which he himself had sent for from Bec. There is no evidence of any other copy in England at this time. Moreover, abridged though it is, all his quotations can be found in it.[1] But the presumption becomes practically a

---

[1] There is one exception. He gives as his authorities for canon 9 of the Council of London the Council of Elvira and the Eleventh Council of Toledo; the latter certainly contains the decree referred to, but the Council of Elvira does not. I think this is simply a misquotation on his part; I can find no evidence of the mistake having been made in any collection from which he could have copied it.

certainty when we notice in letter 26 to bishop Herfast of Thetford, where he quotes from three Councils, that his quotations from the Greek Councils of Nicaea and Antioch are in the *Dionysio-Hadriana* text, while his quotation from Toledo XI is in the normal Isidorian text; this, as I have shown, is the peculiar feature of the Councils in this collection.

There is further evidence still. Against a number of passages in the manuscript a note has been made in the margin, in the form of the letter "a", with a dot on each side showing it to be an abbreviation for a word. These are not all in the same hand. Usually they are in the form of the rustic capital "a" that appears in the manuscript—·Λ·—; sometimes of the small letter —·a·.[1] In all, there are somewhat over 200 passages so marked. My belief is that these were done at Lanfranc's direction, and that they represent the passages he wished to have noted for convenient reference. There are two of his letters (nos. 25 and 26, both to bishop Herfast of Thetford), in which he has been at pains to marshal the canonical authority on the points at issue. The first concerns the deposition of a clerk who has usurped priestly functions, the second maintains the authority of the metropolitan. In the first he gives three authorities—from letters of Popes Eusebius, Leo, and Sylverius; they are

---

[1] I have found this "a" mark in other MSS. of this collection, and also in a few other MSS. of ecclesiastical law, especially those belonging to or copied from Canterbury. I believe that it stands for Attende (note!). In one place on this MS. I have found "Attende" written in full, and also once in another MS. which elsewhere uses an "a" in the margin. Another possible suggestion, which was made to me, is that it stands for "auctoritas".

on pp. 53, 133, and 157 of the manuscript. In the second he quotes from a letter of Pope Boniface, and canons of the Councils of Nicaea, Antioch, and Toledo XI; they are on pp. 110, 221, 233, and 363. All the seven passages which he quotes are noted with an "a" in the margin of the manuscript; and it will be seen that in each letter he has quoted the passages in the order in which they appear in the manuscript. I feel convinced that he had previously caused these notes of reference to be made, and so, when he needed his authorities for certain points, all he had to do was to glance through the passages marked until he had found sufficient authority for his purpose. And I am the more impressed by this view owing to the ease with which I was able to follow him and to find his quotations in the manuscript. I soon found the clue, and it took me comparatively few minutes to discover all seven; without it I might have searched for many hours, because he did not give the names of Popes Eusebius and Boniface but simply referred to the canons and the decrees, nor did he specify from which of the thirteen Councils of Toledo he was quoting.[1]

I picture, then, Lanfranc sitting down to his task of making himself acquainted with the necessary parts

[1] It is true that Lanfranc's quotations are not all quite verbally exact. I do not think much stress can be laid on this; we cannot take it for granted that Lanfranc, unlike Burchard and others, was scrupulously exact in his quotations, nor can we be quite sure that we have an accurate text of his letters. Sometimes, as in the quotation from the Council of Antioch, where he reads at the beginning "Per unamquamque provinciam" instead of "Per singulas regiones", he seems to be making a deliberate correction. His variants, which are not numerous, cannot, I think, be found in any MS.; I am sure he was responsible for them.

of the law of the Church, with a Norman scribe (not always the same one) beside him, who probably read aloud the manuscript to him and at his dictation marked the passages which he wished to be noted for future reference; in one or two cases, especially on page 9, the "a" looks as if it might have been written by Lanfranc himself, to judge from the specimens of his signature that survive. There are a few other notes in the manuscript which may well have been added at this time from his dictation. For instance, the marginal note "Hanc epistolam accepit, cum Becci monachus esset" to the letter of Nicholas II to Lanfranc, written (in the same hand) at the end of part I of the manuscript after the oath of Berengar. This sounds like a personal recollection, as does the note "Hanc epistolam accepit dum Cadomensi coenobio praeesset"[1] attached to the letter he received from Alexander II which follows the Councils (though in a different hand) at the end of part II of the manuscript. This letter is followed by the statement, in yet another hand, that the manuscript had been brought by him from Bec—

Hunc librum dato precio emptum ego Lanfrancus archiepiscopus de Beccensi coenobio in Anglicam terram deferri feci et ecclesiae Christi dedi. Si quis eum de iure praefatae aecclesiae abstulerit, anathema sit—

which certainly reads as if dictated by him. At this point the manuscript must have ended at the time that it was studied and used by Lanfranc. Other

---

[1] Lanfranc uses this same phrase "dum adhuc Cadomensi coenobio praeessem" in a letter to Alexander II (quoted in Böhmer, *Fälschungen*, p. 172).

material has been added later, again by different hands. First, the three letters from the anti-Pope Clement III to Lanfranc,[1] which may possibly have been added by his direction, though if so only at the very end of his life. And, finally, the three forged canons on behalf of monks, which Böhmer attributes to Lanfranc partly because of their appearance in this manuscript; though, from the place they occupy in the manuscript and for other reasons, I feel sure that they were not added until after his death. One more marginal note deserves mention. Against section 44 of the *Capitula Ingilramni* has been written: "Hoc capitulum non est canonicum, sed a secularibus legibus sumptum". The statement is correct, and precisely one that we might expect from Lanfranc, who had been trained in the old civil law. But, inasmuch as the same note appears also on the English manuscripts which contain the complete Decretals, I should infer that it was added by him to the original at Bec, from which both the complete and the abridged copies derive, and was directly copied from there on to this manuscript.

If the inference, that the marginalia to this manuscript were made under his direction, can be accepted, it is of great importance in enabling us to discover the mind of Lanfranc and the passages in the law to which he attached chief weight. It is interesting to notice that he is almost entirely concerned with the general rules of Church discipline, the conduct of a local Church, and the authority of the episcopate, especi-

---

[1] Printed, from this MS., by Liebermann, F., in English Hist. Rev., 1901, vol. XVI, pp. 330–332.

ally of the metropolitan and the primate. He has
avoided marking any of the striking passages in which
the supreme authority of the Pope is emphasised; only
one important matter in this connection, the right of
appeal to Rome, is noted by him. He must have been
conscious in reading through the book of the great
stress laid on papal authority, but this does not seem
to have affected him much in practice; with this I
shall deal in a later chapter. But his mind was
strictly not concerned with that question. I doubt very
much whether he really studied this collection in a
thorough manner at all. He used it for his own purpose, to find authority for the work he had to do, as
metropolitan, in reorganising the Church in England.
The case of bishop Burchard of Worms is exactly
analogous. Burchard had a definite standpoint, which
comes out in the selection of authorities he made for
his *Decretum*; he made extensive use of the False
Decretals, and yet the papal authority, as I have
shown, was given a very limited sphere.

But still it is a fact of the greatest importance that,
in the process of reorganising the Church in England
and of reviving in it the study of ecclesiastical law, the
book that he had to his hand for the purpose was a
copy of the famous False Decretals, which were
deliberately designed to exalt papal authority to the
utmost and were the chief source of the new canonical
collections on the Continent. For it made all the
difference to the future, to the generation that began
under his direction the study of ecclesiastical law. If
the students of ecclesiastical law used this as their
text-book, they would constantly be faced by asser-

tions of papal authority which completely justified the claims constantly being expressed from Rome, and with which practice in England so definitely conflicted. They must have been impressed by the difference between the law of the Church as therein expressed and the practice enforced by royal authority in England. The next point, therefore, to be considered is the extent to which this collection was distributed throughout the country, and whether it became, for others besides Lanfranc, the law-book in general use.

We have seen that Lanfranc was continually referring to the canons and the decrees and enjoining the study of them. The first requisite was to provide books for study, and it may naturally be inferred that, at his instigation, copies would be made of the book on which he himself relied. The evidence of the manuscripts completely bears out this inference. I have no hesitation in affirming that Lanfranc's manuscript is the parent (or, at least, the ancestor) of the ten other English manuscripts of this collection, and, as to the first part, of the four French manuscripts as well; it is the original from which they all derive.

In the first place, as I have already explained, it was really composed of two books, separately compiled from two quite distinct originals, but bound together into one volume. The other English manuscripts were clearly copied from a single volume[1]; there is no trace

[1] With the exception of the Bodleian MS., which contains only the Councils, and the second Hereford MS., which is in two separate volumes. This, however, I believe to have been copied from the other Hereford MS. (I state my reasons for this belief in the Appendix), which is a complete volume.

in any of them of two manuscripts having been bound together, and in some cases the whole manuscript is written in one hand. I have been through them all and find that they contain exactly the same material as is in Lanfranc's book, the same papal letters and the same parts of them; and this is true of the Councils also.

Secondly, part I (the Decretals) of Lanfranc's manuscript shows signs of being a compilation, not a copy; in other words it appears to be the original abridgment. It ends, properly speaking, with Nicholas II's letter to Lanfranc on p. 211. The rest of that page and the remaining pages (212–216) of the last quire have been filled up by letters (previously omitted) of Popes Urban, Dionysius, Sylvester, the letter of Athanasius to Pope Mark, and the Pope's reply.[1] The scribe has been careful to indicate where these letters should be inserted,[2] and in all the other copies they are included in their right place. The crucial fact is that the letter of Pope Mark was too long for the space available, and the last part of it—an important part, not likely to have been omitted otherwise—had to be left out. It is similarly omitted, without the same reason, in all the other copies. It is almost inconceivable that, if these letters added at the end of Lanfranc's manuscript had been originally omitted by the carelessness of the scribe, the space required to

---

[1] This explains the mistake in the Catalogue of MSS. of Trinity College, where it is stated that the decretals end with Mark.

[2] E.g. on p. 39 in the margin between the letters of Calixtus and Antherius—"Desunt decreta Urbani papae, quae invenies in xiiiimo quaternione ad hoc signum ⌒⌒". On p. 211 the letter is given with the direction that it ought to follow Calixtus' decrees, at the place where this sign is to be found.

insert them would have exactly coincided with the
vacant pages at the end of the last quire. The obvious
conclusion is that the writer who made the abridgment discovered that he had just over five pages to
fill, and so decided to add some extra letters; he had
to stop in the middle of Pope Mark's letter, because
he had come to the end of the quire.[1]

Thirdly, there are a number of passages in both
parts of Lanfranc's manuscript where the original text
(apparently the same as that given by Hinschius) has
been erased and a new reading introduced. In every
case the corrected readings appear as the text in all the
other copies, and there is no sign of an erasure. This
by itself seems a clear indication that the other manuscripts were copied from Lanfranc's corrected manuscript; no other explanation of this phenomenon
seems reasonable.

The cumulative evidence is therefore very strong
for my conclusion that Lanfranc's is the parent manuscript. In only one respect do the other manuscripts
fail to produce an almost exact replica of their original.
With the exception of the Peterhouse and Corpus
Christi College manuscripts, they have omitted to
include the additional documents which were already
attached to Lanfranc's book when he made use of it
himself in England—his letters from Nicholas II at
the end of part I and from Alexander II at the end of
part II. But these are personal letters to Lanfranc and
really foreign to the collection; it is hardly strange that

---

[1] The MS. has been numbered by pages. There are 216 pages, or
108 folios, in the first part. The last quire—the 14th—is a complete
quire of 8 folios.

an intelligent scribe should omit them. This additional material, however, has its interest, for it enables us to trace the course of events a little more precisely. The letter from Pope Nicholas follows straight on in the same hand as the rest of part I. It is probable, therefore, that it had already been added to the original manuscript from which the abridgment was made, especially if this original was, as I believe, at Bec. If Lanfranc had had copied on it the documents from the 1059 synod, it is natural that he should also have had copied the letter he received from the Pope while he was at Bec. On the other hand, the letter from Pope Alexander was written to him when he was abbot of Caen, and therefore would not be likely to get onto a Bec manuscript. It is written in a different hand from the Councils that precede it, and more probably was added at Lanfranc's direction after he had received the manuscript from Bec.

Most of what I have said applies to the French copies of this collection as well as to the English. They, too, exactly reproduce all the same material in the right order, and they have the corrected readings where corrections were made in Lanfranc's manuscript. Their exact coincidence seems to indicate again that Lanfranc's was the original abridgment of the Decretals, for which perhaps he was himself responsible when he was at Bec. And the fact that the three twelfth-century French manuscripts, all of Norman origin, contain only the Decretals helps to prove that the two parts of Lanfranc's volume were originally separate manuscripts in the Bec library. I presume that the French manuscripts derive from a copy made from part I before it came to England; this copy might be the *Excerpta Decretorum* of the twelfth-century catalogue. At any rate, I believe that Lanfranc obtained two manuscripts from Bec—the original abridgment of the Decretals and the complete text of the Councils—and had them bound together for use in England. They could spare them both at Bec, for they still had the complete text of the Decretals, from which the abridgment had been made; and I feel sure that they also had a complete text of the Councils, not the same text as the copy bought by Lanfranc, but a normal Isidorian or pseudo-Isidorian version. Of this there is some trace in an Eton manuscript containing the complete text of Decretals and Councils, about which I shall speak in the next chapter.

We are not, however, so much concerned with Normandy as with England, and with the success that attended Lanfranc's introduction of the False Decretals into this country. Of this we can speak with confidence, as his volume had a numerous progeny. This must have been the case, for ten of them still survive in England, and this is a large number to have escaped the fate that befell so many manuscripts, especially old law-books. The number is the more noteworthy because they all appeared within a limited space of time; most of them were written in the late eleventh or early twelfth century, and none later than the twelfth century. But the most remarkable thing about this group of manuscripts is that we are able to trace, with tolerable certainty, almost all of them to their original homes; in only two cases is there no satisfactory clue as to the provenance. The parent manuscript, the one now in Trinity College, Cambridge, was given by Lanfranc to the cathedral church of Canterbury. The one at Peterhouse comes from the cathedral library of Durham. The copy that is in Lincoln cathedral library has been there always; and the same is almost certainly true of the copy in Salisbury cathedral library. Of the two copies in Hereford cathedral library, the second has certainly been there always; the evidence about the first is not so clear, and I cannot help wondering whether it was borrowed in the twelfth century for the purpose of copying and was never returned. Of the three manuscripts in the British Museum, one certainly belonged to Worcester priory, the cathedral church of Worcester; another comes from the famous abbey of Gloucester; as to the third, nothing is known. Nor is there any definite information about the copy in the library of Corpus Christi College, Cambridge, though Dr James thinks that the scribes may have been monks of St Augustine's, Canterbury. Finally, the Bodleian copy, which contains only the Councils, comes from Exeter cathedral library, which was probably its original home; at any rate it was there in bishop Grandison's time, for his familiar handwriting appears in it.

This list reveals the striking information that no less than seven cathedral libraries—and, even after the foundation of Ely, there were only fifteen bishoprics in all—contained a copy of this collection; certainly in the case of five, and most probably in the case of Salisbury and Exeter as well. It is not too extravagant an assumption that there was a copy in every cathedral library for the bishop to use. The presence of a copy in the abbey of Gloucester is equally significant, for Gloucester was one of the three cities that annually saw the Conqueror wearing his crown on the occasion of a great festival of the Church. The official character of this collection stands revealed. And as Lanfranc gave his book to his cathedral library, so too did William of St Carileph to his cathedral library at Durham. We can almost certainly identify the volume of *Decreta Pontificum*, which figures in his donation, with the copy of this collection which is now in the library of Peterhouse.[1]

But the cathedral was not only the seat of the bishop. It was also supposed to be, and often was, a centre of instruction. It is not only important that the judges-ordinary had this book at hand for reference. It is perhaps more important that it was in this way available for the student, the book from which the rising generation would get their knowledge of ecclesiastical law; and, so far as the eleventh century is concerned, I can find no trace of any other book. Also it was, as far as possible, an edition adapted to the use of students. I suggested before that the abridgment of the papal decretals had perhaps been made for this very purpose. And, moreover, most of the letters are divided up into paragraphs which are numbered, and the subject-matter of each paragraph is given in an index which comes at the head of the letter. This certainly facilitated the task of a student

---

[1] Turner, C. H., *The earliest list of Durham MSS.* (Journal of Theological Studies, vol. XIX, pp. 121 foll.).

who wished to discover the law on any particular subject.

There is one such student, a pupil of Lanfranc himself, who, I feel, must be associated with one of the copies of this collection. We are told that bishop Wulfstan of Worcester had a favourite pupil, Nicholas, whom he sent to Canterbury to have his education completed under Lanfranc. This Nicholas returned to Worcester and became prior there; but he kept up his connection with Canterbury, and was in correspondence with Eadmer, the author of the *Historia Novorum*. There is a letter of his to Eadmer, at the beginning of which he quotes from one of the forged decretals.[1] I venture the suggestion that this prior of Worcester may have been responsible for some of the books that were in his cathedral library, for instance, the early twelfth-century copy of Lanfranc's collection, Lanfranc's monastic constitutions, and the Epistles of St Paul with Lanfranc's gloss.[2]

This does not quite conclude the story of this collection. I have found some other traces of it in manuscripts. In the Lincoln cathedral library there is an edition (of the eleventh-twelfth century) of the first four Ecumenical Councils, which I am sure was copied from part II of this collection. There is also a fragment consisting of the first three letters of Pope Clement, the opening letters of the collection, in a Bodleian manuscript which comes from Waltham Abbey. The short titles to the letters and a peculiar

---

[1] Migne, PL. CLIX, col. 809.
[2] For a list of Worcester MSS., see Turner, C. H., *Early Worcester MSS.* (Oxford, 1916).

reading in the first of them,[1] make me confident that
they are derived from this collection; and I believe
this to be true also of the same three letters which
appear in one of the Harleian manuscripts in the
British Museum. But a much more important proof
of the use made of this book is the existence of an
abstract of it, similar to the abstract made in the
Tripartita from the normal edition of the False
Decretals. This takes the form of a collection of
extracts from the decretals followed by extracts from
the Councils. Not only are all the extracts to be
found in Lanfranc's collection, but also the number
given to the extracts from each Pope corresponds
with the numbering of the paragraphs in that collection; furthermore, the extracts from the Greek
Councils are in the *Dionysio-Hadriana* version. From
certain indications I should judge that these extracts
were taken directly from Lanfranc's own copy at
Canterbury.[2] I have found two manuscripts containing this collection of extracts, one in the Lambeth
palace library, the other in the Durham cathedral
library; the latter, which is in the familiar Christ
Church hand, was certainly written at Canterbury.
Moreover, there was once a third copy in the Christ

---

[1] A sentence in the normal text ends " hoc ipsorum est proprium "
(Hinschius, p. 45, two lines from bottom). In Lanfranc's MS.
"proprium" has been erased (leaving a gap) and a stop put after
"est". The other MSS. of this collection, and also the Bodleian and
Harleian MSS. mentioned above, read accordingly "hoc ipsorum
est". This was not the reading of the complete original at Bec, for in
the English MSS. containing the complete Decretals "proprium" is
included.

[2] Especially the interesting fact that the extracts taken from
Urban's letter are misplaced. Cf. above, p. 74, n. 2.

Church library, which is now missing. It appears as no. 1399 in Prior Eastry's catalogue,[1] and the other contents of the volume there described show that it contained exactly the same material as the Durham manuscript. It appears again as no. 220 in Ingram's list,[2] where its 2° fo. incipit is given as *eterna custodienda*. The 2° fo. incipit of the Durham manuscript is *tione eterna custodienda*. So the two books must have been almost facsimiles of one another.[3]

The evidence then shows that this collection brought by Lanfranc from Bec, a collection containing all the important material of the False Decretals, was widely copied, was probably in every cathedral library, and in some monastic libraries as well, and that it was the authoritative collection of Church law in the English Church; during the second half of the eleventh century it was apparently the only collection, and it must, I think, have remained so almost till the middle of the twelfth century, for there is very little else that can definitely be attributed to the early twelfth century. Now it is not only remarkable that so many copies should have been made of this collection in so comparatively limited a space of time. It is also a little curious, perhaps, that no later copies seem to have been made. But, although adapted for the use of students, any collection arranged chronologically and

---

[1] James, M. R., *The Ancient Libraries of Canterbury and Dover*, p. 119.

[2] *Ib.* p. 160.

[3] They are certainly two distinct books. Ingram's list was made in 1508, while the Durham MS. can be identified, with its class mark and its 2° fo. incipit, in the Durham catalogue of 1391. See *Catalogi Veteres* (Surtees Society, vol. VII, 1838).

not according to subject-matter is a difficult one to handle. Lanfranc, as a lawyer, might prefer to have the original sources in his hands. But other people would prefer a systematic collection, where the arrangement had been done for them, and also one that was up-to-date, containing the latest material and not ending in the eighth century. A number of such systematic and up-to-date collections were being made on the Continent, and as they begin to come into England, especially the works of Ivo of Chartres, they soon replace this source-book of the older law. There might still be people who would like to have the old sources as well, but they would like them complete, not abridged; for them the Continent again supplied the material. Lanfranc's collection had had its day. But it had played a most important part in the development of the canon law in England. Lanfranc introduced the collection that he found to his hand at Bec. He was anxious to spread knowledge of the law of the Church, but by introducing this collection he did considerably more than he designed to do. Unwittingly, he sowed the seeds of revolt against that system of Church government which he and his royal master had instituted and maintained.

CHAPTER VI

THE TWELFTH-CENTURY COLLECTIONS

THE history of the development of canon law in England becomes much more complicated when we pass from the eleventh to the twelfth century. It is not that material is lacking, but that the material is so various and cannot be arranged in its proper chronological order. We can only say what the surviving manuscripts show to have been in England in the twelfth century; we cannot say when it came here. We may draw a line between the pre-Gratian collections and Gratian, but that line will not mark a clear-cut division of time. Some of the older collections probably continued to enter the country, and certainly were still being copied, after the arrival of Gratian; it doubtless took a little time for students to discriminate and to recognise that Gratian made the others unnecessary. Ivo's *Pannormia*, at any rate, was so popular that it was still being copied in the thirteenth century. We have to discriminate, too, between the collections which were in general circulation and those which only attained to a limited circulation. Lanfranc's collection, as we have seen, is in the first category; and with it must be included both Ivo and Gratian. It is only these two authors that, for the same period, hold this position on the Continent also. The other collections, in England as elsewhere, are confined to a few libraries only. I want to show what material was made available for English use, and in particular how far the collections that were current, whether universally or locally, on the Continent were also current in England. The best way of doing this is to arrange them in the order of their original appearance, and I hope it will be clear that this is not necessarily the order in which they came into England. Some travelled more slowly than others, but the thing that matters is that all, at any rate all that were important on the Continent, did arrive, and were here in the twelfth century.[1]

i. *The False Decretals* (complete).

The English Church after the Conquest started, like the rest of the Church in the eleventh century, though a trifle later, with the False Decretals as the basis of its law. At first, it is true, the decretals were in an abridged edition, but the abridgment was not important as the essential character of the collection remained intact. By the middle of the twelfth century complete copies of the False Decretals had come into this country, and two twelfth-century manuscripts are still in existence—one, coming from Canterbury and written in the Christ Church hand, is now in the British Museum; the other, of unknown provenance, is in the Eton College library. The former contains the decretals only; in the latter the decretals are followed by the Councils. Each of these manuscripts has its fifteenth-century counterpart. The Canterbury manuscript has been exactly copied in a manuscript in

---

[1] In the following pages I am principally concerned with showing how much material was available in England in the twelfth century. A more precise description of the various MSS. of each collection will be found in the Appendix.

Cambridge University Library; and there is a manuscript in the British Museum which must, I think,
have been copied (at first or second hand) from the
Eton manuscript.[1]

As far as the decretals are concerned, these manuscripts contain the same material up to Gregory I,
arranged in the same order,[2] and prefaced by the same
index ending with "Decreta Nicholai" (i.e. the documents from the 1059 synod). But while the contents
of the Eton manuscript correspond with the index,[3]
those of the Canterbury manuscript do not. The reason for this is that the last scribe in the Canterbury
book, who wrote from Gregory I onwards, introduced, in their correct chronological order, all the
papal letters that he could discover at Canterbury,
including the famous "Lanfranc" forgeries. It is
quite clear, however, that the two manuscripts derive
from the same original; and this original, since it
contained the documents of the 1059 synod, was
doubtless at Bec. Moreover, the decretals in Lanfranc's
collection must have been abridged from the same
original Bec manuscript; for they are arranged in the
same order and they contain nothing that is not in the
Canterbury and Eton manuscripts. There is another
curious link, in the passages I spoke of where corrections have been made in Lanfranc's manuscript. In
one or two instances the same corrections have been

[1] I have to thank Dr M. R. James for calling my attention to the
Eton MS. It was not known to Hinschius or Böhmer, both of whom
describe the other three MSS.

[2] The arrangement of Leo I's letters differs from the normal, and
some of his and of Gregory I's letters are omitted.

[3] Except that the 1079 oath of Berengar is included in the text.

made in the Canterbury manuscript, leaving the original text partly visible. In most cases Lanfranc's corrected reading is the substantive text of both the Canterbury and Eton manuscripts, though in a few instances they have the original and not the corrected text. Possibly the Bec original contained a number of corrected readings in the margin, which were not always noticed, or not noticed at once, by the scribes. But, whatever is the explanation of this phenomenon, it is at any rate further evidence that all these manuscripts derive from a common original, which was at Bec in Lanfranc's time.

Now, while the first part of the Eton manuscript (and likewise of its fifteenth-century copy in the British Museum) falls exactly into line with all the other English manuscripts of the False Decretals, the second part does not. It is a normal Isidorian version of the Councils, containing the material that is regularly found in a normal text of the False Decretals, and therefore differing considerably from the peculiar version of the Councils in Lanfranc's manuscript. This is quite intelligible if the copy which Lanfranc brought to England was the only one of its kind at Bec; the presumption is that there remained at Bec another text of the Councils which was copied onto the Eton manuscript. It is prefaced by an index not only of the Councils but also of the genuine papal decretals which follow the Councils in the genuine Isidorian collection known as the *Hispana*. The decretals are not copied in the text; they had already appeared in the first part of the manuscript. But it may be noted that there is evidence, which I shall mention in the next two sections of this chapter, of the use of the *Hispana* in two compilations which came into England at this time.

The Eton manuscript is described by Dr James as written in a very fine hand, possibly French. A number of manuscripts containing canonical collections, which were almost certainly in England in the twelfth century, appear to have been written in N. France. There was certainly a heightened interest in the subject of canon law, and a desire to get more material for its study. Who was the moving spirit in this? The appearance in the mid-twelfth century of two manuscripts of the False Decretals deriving from a Bec original makes us think at once of Theobald, the abbot of Bec who became archbishop of Canterbury in 1139. We know that he was an expert in the canon law himself, and that he instructed his household in it. The influx of manuscripts containing new collections of ecclesiastical law seems to date from the time of his archbishopric; before it there is practically no evidence of anything besides Lanfranc's collection. Theobald, then, probably played the part in the twelfth century that Lanfranc had played in the eleventh, in encouraging the study of the law and in providing material for the study; though the material is now more varied and more up-to-date. And there is an important distinction to be drawn. Theobald started with an entirely different standpoint from that of Lanfranc on the vital question of Church government and papal authority.

ii. *The* Decretum *of Burchard of Worms.*

In the first half of the eleventh century the collection most prevalent on the Continent had been the *Decretum* of Burchard. It does not seem to have penetrated into England at that time, and it was only in the twelfth century, when it was already out-of-date on the Continent, that it came in at the same time as other and more modern collections. There are two manuscripts which, though apparently of foreign origin, were probably in this country in the twelfth century. One is in Durham cathedral library; the other is in the British Museum, and may have come from Canterbury as the material bound up with it certainly did. There is further evidence of the existence of manuscripts of Burchard; for instance, in a manuscript at St John's College, Oxford, of the *Pannormia* of Ivo of Chartres, which had been correctly copied down to the middle of book VII; but in the place of the remainder of book VII and of book VIII another scribe, doubtless mistaking the original from which he was supposed to copy, has written book VII and part of book VIII of Burchard. Also there is an interesting twelfth-century manuscript in the Hereford cathedral library, really in two parts, in both of which the main ingredient is an abstract of Burchard. The second part is much the fuller and the more important. In the early books the compiler has added a large number of extracts from other sources, while in the later books there is very little besides Burchard; but in place of book XVIII of Burchard he has inserted a collection of 164 canons, mainly of Councils, which seem to derive partly from a manuscript of the *Dionysio-Hadriana*, partly from the *Hispana*.[1] On the whole, though the name of Burchard seems to have been as familiar to canonists in England as elsewhere, his work, probably owing to its late arrival, seems to have been little used. The Durham manuscript was actually ascribed to Ivo of Chartres in the medieval library catalogues.

iii. *The new Roman collections of the eleventh century.*

Burchard's was obviously an unsatisfactory book for the reformed Papacy engaged in the task of ecclesiastical centralisation under its own direct control. As I described above,[2] the re-statement of canon law begins with the appearance about 1050 of a *Collection in 74 Titles*, based on the False Decretals and the letters of Gregory I. M. Fournier has shown that this collection spread even outside Italy, and that its influence is felt on all later collections. It penetrated into England also. There is a manuscript of it in the Canterbury cathedral library, which was probably there already in the twelfth century, bearing the usual heading "Diversorum patrum sententiae de primatu Romanae ecclesiae". This is a copy considerably enlarged, and re-arranged in three books; but it is an indubitable copy of the *Collection in 74 Titles*. A fourth book, a very unusual collection mainly of later Councils, has been added, and also a fifth book containing 120 canons showing considerable affinities with the similar col-

---

[1] The last 45 of these canons are abstracts from the three parts of the *Dacheriana* (see note 1 on the next page).

[2] Introduction, chapter III.

lection inserted in the Hereford manuscript of Burchard, and like them derived apparently from the
Dionysio-Hadriana and the *Hispana*.[1]

Of the collections made during Gregory VII's
papacy, only one had any vogue outside Rome—that
of Anselm of Lucca. I have discovered a twelfth-
century copy of this in the library of Corpus Christi
College, Cambridge, which has lain concealed under
the title "Summa totius iuris canonici" ever since it
was presented to the library by Archbishop Parker.
Like all the manuscripts of Anselm, the Corpus manuscript is written in an Italian hand. Unfortunately
there is no clue as to when it came into England; we
only know that in the fifteenth century it belonged to
the Cistercian abbey of Pipewell in Northampton-
shire, an abbey famous in Richard I's reign as the
scene of a notable Council at which a number of
ecclesiastical appointments were made. It is probable
that this book, important still in the twelfth century,
would not have travelled much in the later Middle
Ages.

iv. *Collections of abstracts.*

These early compilers left a permanent impression upon the law of the Church, and the object of the
Popes was completely achieved by them. There followed a period of less tendencious and more scientific
compilation, in which, as I have already suggested,
the writers were not satisfied merely with adding to

---

[1] Since writing the above, I have discovered that this series of
120 canons is actually part I of the collection in three parts published by L. d'Achery in his *Spicilegium*, vol. I, pp. 539-564 (Paris,
1723); this collection is usually known as the *Dacheriana*.

former collections. They first of all went back to the original sources and made their own abstracts, putting titles to them to facilitate re-arrangement, and then added material from the work of their predecessors. A feature of such abstracts, of which English manuscripts in particular provide examples, is that they regularly begin with extracts, in their right order, from the False Decretals and the Councils, which are usually followed by extracts from the letters of Gregory I. I have already mentioned the abstract of Lanfranc's collection that was made in England, of which we possess two copies and have evidence of a third;[1] it is followed in the manuscripts by extracts from each of the fourteen books of Gregory I's *Register*. In the Hereford manuscript of Burchard the compiler has at one point inserted over 100 extracts from forged decretals, in their proper order; and in the Canterbury manuscript of the *Collection in 74 Titles* there is evidence that the compiler of this enlarged edition went back to the sources—the False Decretals and Gregory I—and was not content merely to transcribe the exact words of his original.

In many cases the material would have been collected in this way with a view to the formation of a collection arranged according to subject-matter, and when this had been done the original abstracts would probably have been destroyed. Some have survived; in particular, there is one collection of which M. Fournier has found seventeen manuscripts on the Continent—a collection in three parts known usually as the *Tripartita* or *Collectio trium partium*, which was

---

[1] See above, pp. 81-82.

perhaps formed by Ivo of Chartres and is at any rate the basis of his later collections.[1] I have discovered two manuscripts of this collection in England. One is in my own College library at Caius, a manuscript not described by Dr James, because it was apparently missing when he made his catalogue; it was written in England in the twelfth century, probably in the first half of the century. The other copy, also of the twelfth century, is in the Bodleian; the handwriting seems to be northern French rather than English, but otherwise it is very similar to the Caius manuscript, and they both of them differ in certain respects from the one described by M. Fournier.

An apparent copy of the abstract of the False Decretals contained in the *Tripartita* has recently been discovered in a Bruges manuscript.[2] I have found a duplicate of this in a British Museum manuscript written in a foreign, possibly German, hand. But I am not clear that it really is a copy of the *Tripartita*. Certainly it does contain the usual introduction, but it is divided into three parts—early decretals, Councils, later decretals—as an ordinary manuscript of the False Decretals is, while the *Tripartita* has all the decretals before the Councils; also the second and third parts of this collection have a separate introduction not to be found in the *Tripartita*. Moreover, at best it is an abridgment and not a copy. It seems to me much more like an earlier attempt at an abstract of the False

---

[1] See above, p. 40.
[2] Poorter, A. De and Brys, J., *Les manuscrits de droit médiéval de l'ancienne abbaye des Dunes à Bruges* (Revue d'histoire ecclésiastique, vol. XXVI, pp. 611–612. Louvain, 1930).

Decretals, of which the *Tripartita* represents an improved and more complete version. Finally, I have found yet another twelfth-century manuscript in the British Museum[1], which closely resembles part I of the *Tripartita*. It seems to me to be an independent compilation, but made from the same sources that were used by the author of the *Tripartita*. It differs in many respects, and notably in that it has a different selection from the letters of Gregory I and also contains a much larger selection from the Boniface correspondence. It looks, therefore, as if there was more than one person engaged on the same task of making these preliminary abstracts; possibly they lived in the same region, as they seem to have employed more or less the same material. They were probably not working in England, as it is from a complete copy of the False Decretals containing the normal text of the Councils that these abstracts were made.

v. *Ivo of Chartres.*

This work of abstracting, whether done by himself or by others, was at any rate put to good use by bishop Ivo of Chartres just before the close of the eleventh century. It was certainly the *Tripartita*, together with the writings of the Fathers and the *Decretum* of Burchard, that he principally employed in the compilation of his own *Decretum*, a large work arranged

---

[1] On a fly-leaf this is stated, in a twelfth-century hand, to have been given to the priory of Cirencester in the first half of the twelfth century. The MS. does not seem to have been written quite so early as that. Perhaps this fly-leaf was originally attached to some other MS.

according to subjects and divided into seventeen parts. Of this work M. Fournier could only discover six manuscripts, one of which, now in the British Museum, was originally in Lincoln cathedral library; he was unaware of the copy in the library of Corpus Christi College, Cambridge, which comes from Christ Church, Canterbury. So actually two of the seven known copies of Ivo's *Decretum* are English. There is in the British Museum a copy of the abridgment of this work in sixteen parts, but it is of foreign origin and probably of later importation. The *Decretum* did not have much vogue, because Ivo soon replaced it by a shorter and better work in eight books—the *Pannormia*. This, as I have said, became popular everywhere, and was the collection which had the widest circulation before Gratian. Ivo's writings were well known in England. His letters and sermons figure in numerous manuscripts, and I have found several copies of the *Pannormia*. One of these, at Jesus College, Oxford, is in an early twelfth-century English hand, so that the work did not take long to reach England; on the other hand, some of the manuscripts were written in the thirteenth century, and it is a tribute to Ivo's reputation that his book continued to be copied more than half a century after Gratian had come into this country. Finally, I should add that an enlargement of the *Pannormia* in ten books has been described by M. Fournier, who knew of four continental manuscripts. To these must be added again a twelfth-century copy at Corpus Christi College, also deriving from Canterbury.

vi. *Anonymous compilations.*

This does not quite complete the tale of pre-Gratian collections in this country. In a number of manuscripts one comes across various small collections, as one does in all parts of Europe, which cannot be fitted precisely into any of the categories I have mentioned. No two of these compilations are exactly alike, though they often have a number of canons in common; but put them all together and there is probably no canon in the whole mass that cannot be found in one of the collections that I have enumerated. It is as one would expect. Individuals collected for their own purposes, not for general publication, some of the chief canons bearing on questions that were continually cropping up or that affected themselves personally—the rules governing the lives and property of the monks, the lives of the secular clergy, disputed points arising out of the sacraments of baptism and marriage, and so on. The compiler was not satisfied with the list in one collection; he took the two or more collections that were available to him and amalgamated the canons in them all. The False Decretals and the canons of Councils are the original sources of most of these extracts, but probably they are usually copied actually out of some later collection. These individual compilations are by no means always derived from pre-Gratian material. In some of them Gratian was probably the chief source, though not usually the only one; on the other hand, abstracts of Gratian are quite common. But we can derive some positive evidence from these anonymous note-books. They indicate that the collections of ecclesiastical law that I have described must have been found in English libraries in the twelfth century in larger numbers than existing manuscripts would lead us to infer.

Naturally, as I said before, old and out-of-date lawbooks would not have a very good chance of survival, apart from the fate that many of them must have suffered at the Reformation, and the ravages of neglect in medieval as well as in modern times. But anyhow quite a representative selection has survived. Of these, in only a limited number of cases do we know the libraries that originally possessed them, but it is worth while to take a few of the cathedral libraries and to note, from the evidence which I have already given, what pre-Gratian collections they possessed in the twelfth century. Thus, Christ Church, Canterbury, had a complete copy of the False Decretals; it also had Lanfranc's collection, the *Decretum* of Burchard, the *Collection in 74 Titles* in an amplified form, the *Decretum* of Ivo, and an enlarged edition of Ivo's *Pannormia*. Hereford had two copies of Lanfranc's collection, an abridged Burchard, and a copy of the *Pannormia*. Lincoln had a copy of Lanfranc's collection, and both the *Decretum* and *Pannormia* of Ivo. Durham had a copy of Lanfranc's collection, an abridgment of it, and also a copy of Burchard. And this evidence comes solely from manuscripts which have survived to the present day and of which we actually know the provenance.

I have dealt in this chapter solely with pre-Gratian material. It hardly seems necessary to pursue my

enquiry further, to the new period which opens with
the appearance of Gratian's *Decretum*. Written about
1140, it must have come into England, as I shall
presently show, very soon after the middle of the
twelfth century. It was followed, later in the century,
by unofficial collections of papal decretals of the
second half of the century, which were compiled in
England more eagerly and successfully than anywhere
else. These individual collections were superseded in
the thirteenth century by the official *Decretales* of
Gregory IX, to which considerable additions were
made by later Popes. Together they combine with
Gratian's *Decretum* to make up the Corpus Juris
Canonici; and there can be no doubt that this was the
authoritative Code of Canon Law in England, as well
as at Rome and elsewhere. Large numbers of manuscripts of the *Decretum* and of the *Decretales* survive.
They must have been in every medieval library, and
important libraries had several copies. Thus, in the
catalogue of the library of Christ Church, Canterbury,
in prior Eastry's time (at the beginning of the fourteenth century), we can see that there were ten or
twelve copies of the *Decretum* and at least as many of
the *Decretales*. The fifteenth-century catalogue of St
Augustine's, Canterbury, shows a similar number in
the library of that monastery.

The evidence from surviving manuscripts seems to
me to point to a definite conclusion, which is not
likely to be affected by any further discoveries that
may be made. All the collections that were at all prevalent on the Continent are found to have been in
this country also, and the English Church seems to

have had its full share of the extant canonical literature. It started, like the rest of the Church, with the
great source-book, the False Decretals, and no country
was better equipped in this respect. It then acquired
the new systematic collections, even some of those that
seemed particularly Roman; but especially the works
of Ivo of Chartres, and then the *Decretum* of Gratian,
which arrived at quite an early date. The range of its
acquisitions is impressive; there seems no real gap. It
had all the canons that upheld the papal sovereignty
of the Church, and it was up-to-date in its possession
of recent decrees of Popes and the canons of recent
Councils. The signs of study, too, are manifest in the
abstracts made from the False Decretals and other
sources, and in the compilations that individuals made
for their own use. On the other hand, it had nothing
distinctively its own. We are accustomed to hear that
the English Church selected from the canons of the
Roman Church such as it thought fit to accept. If so,
some record must have been kept of that selection, or
no one would have known what law to follow. We
should expect to find several manuscripts of it. On
the contrary, there is not the slightest trace of a special
collection selected for the use of the English Church
in any manuscript, in any medieval library catalogue,
in any contemporary writer. Clearly it did not exist.
The English Church was subject to the same laws, to
all the same laws, that the rest of the Church obeyed.

The tale of twelfth-century collections of law does
not exhaust the evidence to be derived from manuscripts. There is something further, of a rather differ-

ent character. A supporter of the older view, championed by Stubbs, would probably lay more weight on the conciliar legislation of the English Church than on the law-books that it possessed. It has been held that the English Church legislated for itself in its Councils, and in them selected only such canons of the Roman Church as it thought fit to adopt. It might be urged that they used the law-books for this purpose only. This view, however, is based on a mistaken idea of conciliar legislation, which has been carried further and applied to Church Councils in general. It has been argued (in modern times) that only a canon debated and agreed upon at a Council was binding on the Church; this theory has been applied, for instance, to the Fourth Lateran Council, with fantastic results. Such a view could never have been advanced in the twelfth century. The canon law of the Church was built up on the decrees of Popes as well as upon the canons of Councils; in fact, in all the systematic collections of which I have spoken the decrees largely outnumber the canons. And when we turn to the Councils of the Church in the eleventh and twelfth centuries, numerous and important as they are, we find that they deal on the whole with a very limited range of subjects, and that they are frequently merely repeating older decrees and canons, sometimes quoting them as their authority. Not all the details of Church government and judicial administration are discussed, but only certain points which come prominently to the front, especially abuses that need immediately to be remedied; these were dealt with again and again. To a greater degree still is this true of

England. The range of subjects dealt with is very small; a few points, the most important being clerical marriage, are constantly repeated. The Councils did not attempt, did not even make a beginning towards, the creation of a code of Church law. A Council was an effective way of calling attention to the abuses within the Church, of getting general assent to the remedying of them, and, above all, of putting on the participants the onus of doing their share in enforcing the laws—the old laws—against these abuses. Similar to the desire of the king in England in the thirteenth century for fuller representation in his Parliaments was the desire of the Pope, notably of Innocent III at the Fourth Lateran Council, for his Councils to be as representative as possible. He did not need them for the passing of laws, which he could promulgate of his own authority; he, and not the Council, was the source of law.

But though the older view is both mistaken and misleading, it is worth while to take it seriously for a moment and to review the Councils that were held in England from the Conquest onwards. It is not necessary to go farther back, because there was no collection of earlier Councils and the practice of holding them had fallen into disuse. I have made a list of the English Councils up to the end of the twelfth century of which the canons have been preserved in manuscripts, and I believe the list to be a complete one. Mostly I have found them written in on spare pages of a manuscript, especially a manuscript containing a collection of ecclesiastical law; obviously it was desired to keep record of them. I have found a number of

copies of most of them, and at least four copies of all
of them; I am speaking of canons of Councils written
separately onto manuscripts, not of those which are
recorded by chroniclers. There are in all nine of them,
and they are all Councils of the whole English Church.
First come the two most important of Lanfranc's
Councils—at London in 1075 and Winchester in
1076; then Anselm's two Councils in 1102 and 1108.
Both Lanfranc and Anselm could summon general
Councils of the whole English Church because of their
primatial authority over York. After Anselm's death,
the archbishops of Canterbury lost this authority, and
there were two separate provinces with separate con-
vocations as at the present day. The English Church
could only be united by papal authority, and the other
five Councils are all legatine Councils. They are: the
Council held by John of Crema, legate *a latere*, in
1125; by archbishop William as papal legate in 1127;
by Alberic, legate *a latere*, in 1138; by bishop Henry
of Winchester as papal legate in 1143; and by archbishop Richard as papal legate in 1175. Not only
were these five Councils all legatine Councils, but the
decrees they promulgated were in pursuance of the
reforms ardently advocated at Rome, and the wording
was in many cases copied from decrees of papal
Councils. This is true also of the Councils held by
Anselm, as might have been expected of so obedient
a servant of the Papacy. In the case of Lanfranc, in
1075 at any rate, there is a difference. But he was then
dealing with a very backward Church, and attempting
in his canons to bring it up to the level of the Church
as a whole; moreover, he is careful to quote his

authorities, which are almost all derived from the pseudo-Isidorian collection in his possession.

There is a tenth Council that can be added from another source. Henry of Huntingdon speaks of a Council presided over by archbishop Theobald in 1151, which was distinguished by an outbreak of appeals to Rome, an unfortunate precedent in the writer's opinion. There is a manuscript in the Bibliothèque Nationale at Paris[1] of Henry of Huntingdon, written between 1170 and 1180, which breaks off in the year 1147 and then adds the canons of the Council of 1151 presided over by archbishop Theobald, papal legate. There are eight canons, directed mainly against the possession or violation of Church property by laymen. They are doubtless genuine, so that we have here another English Council, again a legatine Council.

Most, though not all, of these Councils are to be found with their canons in the writings of contemporary chroniclers. Some other Councils are mentioned by the chroniclers without record of particular canons. The only additions to my list compiled from manuscripts are to be found in Roger of Howden, who records the canons of two Councils held by archbishop Hubert Walter. These again are both of them legatine Councils. The first was at York in 1195, and it is obvious that he could only preside over a Council in the northern province by virtue of his authority as

[1] MS. Bibl. Nat. Latin 6042. The canons of this Council are given in Mansi, *Concilia*, vol. XXI, quoted from Baluzius who took them from this MS. They are not given in Wilkins. I have to thank Mr C. R. Cheney of Wadham College, Oxford, for calling my attention to this MS.

papal legate. The second was at London in 1200, and in its decrees his legatine capacity is clearly betokened. The Third Lateran Council is quoted as authority for most of the decrees; moreover, every canon ends with the words "salvo in omnibus sacrosanctae Romanae ecclesiae honore et privilegio".

This completes the tale of the English Councils of which the canons have been preserved. There is no sign of any attempt to create a body of English Church law. All that was happening was that the English Church, united by papal authority in the person of the legate, was performing a normal function of ecclesiastical government, and was passing decrees conformable with, and often directly derived from, the recent decrees of the Roman Church. These were all Councils of the whole English Church; not until the thirteenth century was any record kept of provincial or diocesan synods. But there are a number of other Councils of which the canons have been preserved in English manuscripts—Councils presided over by the Popes. Of the four great Lateran Councils, I have found the canons of the First (1123), the Third (1179), and the Fourth (1215); the Second (1139) I have not found, but it is echoed to some extent in the English Council of 1143. Besides these greater Councils, later to be included among the Ecumenical Councils, I have found the canons of other papal Councils: for instance, Urban II's at Clermont in 1095, Calixtus II's at Rheims in 1119, Eugenius III's at Rheims in 1148, Alexander III's at Tours in 1163; apparently those Councils at which English ecclesiastics were present have been recorded. I have not attempted to make a complete list, but those that I have mentioned show that the canons of almost all the most important papal Councils were preserved in English documents. So the evidence from Councils, English and papal, is completely in agreement with the evidence provided by the manuscript collections of ecclesiastical law. It equally helps to prove that the law of the Church, the whole law and not a selected part of it, was the law of the English Church.

CHAPTER VII

MEDIEVAL LIBRARIES AND CONTEMPORARY WRITERS

So far I have dealt with manuscripts only. Aided by the information we have obtained from them, we can consider the two other possible sources of evidence—the catalogues of medieval libraries, and the quotations from ecclesiastical law that appear, especially in the letters of contemporaries.

Unfortunately we possess the catalogues of few medieval libraries, and only a small number of these are as early as the twelfth century. However, the evidence from such early catalogues as survive agrees entirely with the evidence derived from manuscripts. To give one or two examples. We have seen that surviving manuscripts show that in the twelfth century Lincoln possessed a copy of Lanfranc's collection and both the *Decretum* and *Pannormia* of Ivo of Chartres. The twelfth-century catalogue shows that there was a copy of Gratian also. Durham, we saw, possessed a copy of Lanfranc's collection, an abridgment of it, and a copy of Burchard; the twelfth-century catalogue mentions these three (though Burchard's work is attributed to Ivo) and includes also a copy of Ivo and a volume of *Exceptiones Decretorum*, probably an abridgment of Gratian. A less important library—that of Whitby Abbey—in the time of abbot Richard (1148–1175) possessed a copy of *Decreta Pontificum* (perhaps Lanfranc's collection), the *Pannormia* of Ivo, and an abridgment of Gratian. Speaking generally, Ivo is everywhere, a copy of Lanfranc's collection is usual, often we find volumes of abstracts, rarely a copy of Burchard. While, if the catalogue was made in the second half of the twelfth century, Gratian is sure to be included, and copies of his work and of the *Decretales* soon become numerous in every library. I quoted before from the libraries of Christ Church and St Augustine's at Canterbury, and I should like to give one or two more instances. We have a list of books that were written at Peterborough during the rule of abbot Benedict (1177–1193). They include two copies of Gratian, two Summae on the *Decretum*, and three copies of *Decretales Epistolae* (i.e. collections of post-Gratian papal decretals prior to the official *Decretales* of Gregory IX). At Reading in the time of Henry III there were five copies of Gratian. At Bury St Edmund's, during the riot of 1327, the mob looted the property of the monastery and seized a number of books; the hated law-books were naturally an object of their fury (another reason which makes it surprising how many have managed to survive), and we learn that they seized seven copies of *Decreta* and ten copies of *Decretales*, which shows that St Edmund's library had been well supplied.[1]

This leads me to a short digression. The *Decreta* plundered by the mob were clearly copies of Gratian.

---

[1] The Lincoln catalogue is quoted in the preface to R. M. Woolley's *Catalogue of MSS. in Lincoln Cathedral Chapter Library*; Durham in *Catalogi Veteres* (Surtees Soc. vol. VII, pp. 1 foll.); Whitby in Charlton's *History of Whitby*, pp. 112–114; Peterborough in Sparke's *Historiae Anglicanae Scriptores Varii*, vol. II, p. 98; Reading in Coates' *History and Antiquities of Reading*, supplement; Bury in James, M. R., *On the Abbey of St Edmund at Bury* (Cambridge Antiquarian Society, 8vo publications, no. XXVIII, p. 108).

From these medieval catalogues we can see that the regular term for a collection of early Church law—the old law—was *Decreta*. If it was a chronological collection such as the False Decretals, whether complete or abridged as in Lanfranc's collection, it will usually be called *Decreta* (or *Excerpta Decretorum*) *Pontificum* (or *Pontificum Romanorum*). In the case of Ivo's works, they are almost always called *Decreta Ivonis*, though in most cases his *Pannormia* and not his *Decretum* is meant. Finally, we have the *Decreta Gratiani*, which is usually referred to, as at Bury, as *Decreta*. *Decreta* by itself seems always to mean what we call the *Decretum* of Gratian; this is certainly always shown to be so when a catalogue entry can be identified in an existing manuscript. Gratian's book became in fact the one compilation of early law, or *decreta*, that everybody used. With it is regularly associated the *Decretales*, the supplement of later papal decretals and canons published by Gregory IX, to which later Popes added other supplements. *Decreta* and *Decretales* go together, because together they make up the corpus of canon law. So, when archbishop Arundel in his *Constitutio* in the fourteenth century details the list of authorities that must be accepted, he starts with *Decreta* and *Decretales*, and there can be no doubt to what he was referring. So too when Lyndwood in his *Provinciale* uses the phrase "in corpore decretorum et decretalium".[1] I mention this, because the words have frequently been misinterpreted.

---

[1] Cf. Maitland, F. W., *Roman Canon Law in the Church of England*, pp. 17 and 47. There is a clearer case still on p. 416 of the Rolls Series edition of the *Fasciculi Zizaniorum*.

The evidence from libraries is, on the whole, slight, but, such as it is, it is quite definite. It exactly falls into line with the evidence derived from existing manuscripts, and provides no trace of any peculiarly English collection. The known collections, which we have found in English manuscripts, are there, but nothing else at all. When we investigate the third possible source, quotations from ecclesiastical law by contemporary writers, we have to deplore both the rarity of their quotations and the uncertainty as to the actual book or books from which they are quoting. However, there is again a certain amount of definite evidence, and the canons they quote are regularly to be found in one or more of the collections I have cited.

We can definitely say that Lanfranc, when he cited ecclesiastical law, was quoting from the copy of the False Decretals which he had bought from Bec. It is almost certain that it was with a copy of the same book (presented by him later to his cathedral library) that William of St Carileph, bishop of Durham, confronted Lanfranc and the Council, and justified his appeal to Rome. And Nicholas, prior of Worcester, a former pupil of Lanfranc, when he quoted one of the early decretals in a letter to Eadmer of Canterbury, was probably quoting from the copy of the same book which we know to have been at Worcester. A little later we find archbishop Ralph of Canterbury making a number of quotations in his long letter to Calixtus II in defence of the privileges of Canterbury. Most of these come from Gregory the Great, whose letters, both complete and abridged, are to be found in a number of English manuscripts in the twelfth century. But he also has three other quotations, two from papal letters and a canon of a Council at Toledo, which are all to be found in Ivo's *Decretum*, and, I think, nowhere else; except possibly in the *Tripartita*, which was Ivo's chief source.

After this there is a gap of over thirty years, when we come to the time of archbishop Theobald and the letters written for him by John of Salisbury. In two consecutive letters (nos. 67 and 68) there are a number of quotations from ecclesiastical law, and I feel sure that the book out of which they were taken was Gratian's *Decretum*. In the first letter there is one quotation which I have not so far been able to track down in any collection;[1] otherwise, the remaining four quotations in that letter and the four quotations in the next letter are all to be found in Gratian; no other collection has them all. Moreover, the quotations in the second letter are all close together in Distinctio 81 of Gratian. If this conclusion is correct, it is definite proof that Gratian's book was already in use in England in Theobald's household by or just before the year 1160. And the evidence from medieval catalogues also indicated that copies of Gratian were in this country quite early in the second half of the twelfth century.

When we come to the great Becket controversy, ecclesiastical law is freely quoted by both sides, and here again, judging by the same tests that were applied

---

[1] He says: "beatus Eugenius in simili causa diffinivit...". I think he may be referring to a dictum of Eugenius III, in whose chancery he had worked. He uses the same phrase to describe Eugenius III in a later letter (*Materials for the history of Archbishop Thomas Becket*, Rolls Series, vol. VII, p. 528).

to John of Salisbury, the source seems usually to be Gratian. This certainly seems true of Becket himself, at any rate after he had retired to the monastery of Pontigny, when quotations from canon law become frequent in his letters[1]; we know that he devoted himself there to the study of the law of the Church, and doubtless he found a copy of Gratian in the monastic library. On the other side, Gilbert Foliot certainly seems to have used Gratian[2]; he was learned in the law, and in earlier days had quoted from the civil as well as the canon law. Another opponent of Becket, bishop Jocelin of Salisbury, seems to have used Ivo of Chartres[3]; possibly the *Pannormia*, though more probably the *Tripartita*, in which the first three of his five quotations appear consecutively. The letters in this controversy show both sides employing the same collections, and those the authoritative ones in the Church as a whole; moreover, while the texts adduced by Becket and his supporters are particularly representative of the views of ecclesiastical authority and Church government which the Papacy was trying to enforce universally, no attempt is made by the other side to deny their validity or their competence in England. It is not Becket's law but his facts that they controvert, and they appeal to the Pope against his sentences.

Apart from this controversy, I have noted in three other writers quotations from canon law. One of them is Bartholomew, bishop of Exeter from 1161 to 1184, whose *Penitentiale* must have been widely read since

---

[1] Cf. *Materials for...Becket*, vol. v, pp. 270 foll. and 393 foll.
[2] *Ib.* pp. 531 foll.   [3] *Ib.* pp. 414 foll.

several manuscripts of it survive; it has never been published or even described. He quotes largely from canon law, and where I have checked his quotations, especially on such a question as simony, I have no doubt at all that Gratian was his chief source. Secondly, archbishop Richard of Canterbury, who in a letter to three other English bishops[1] makes extensive quotations from canon law, all apparently out of Gratian. In one place, where he uses the phrase "in corpore decretorum", he seems to be actually naming his source. Finally, Ralph de Diceto, writing at the end of the twelfth century, quotes at length from the preface which Ivo of Chartres attached both to the *Decretum* and the *Pannormia*, and, later, on three occasions adduces this as his authority on points of ecclesiastical law[2]; he definitely quotes his source. Ralph is clearly not in sympathy with the advanced reformers, but he uses an orthodox law-book.

This concludes my consideration of the evidence that can be obtained from three different sources: existing manuscripts, medieval catalogues, and contemporary quotations. I do not pretend that I have exhausted the evidence; especially was it impossible for me to be sure that I had not overlooked some manuscripts. But I have discovered ample evidence

---

[1] *Materials for...Becket*, Rolls Series, vol. VII, pp. 561 foll. Cf. Pollock and Maitland, *History of English Law*, vol. I, 2nd ed. p. 457. Also Seckel, E., *Die Westminster-Synode*, 1175 (Deutsche Ztsch. für Kirchenrecht, 3 Folge, vol. IX, pp. 159–189. Freiburg-i.-B., 1899), has shown that Gratian was the chief source of the decrees of Richard's Council of 1175.

[2] Ralph de Diceto, *Opera historica*, ed. Stubbs, W. Rolls Series, vol. II, pp. 32–3, 298, 305, 413.

to enable me to arrive at a perfectly definite conclusion, which can hardly be affected by any further discoveries. The English Church recognised the same law as the rest of the Church; it possessed and used the same collections of Church law that were employed in the rest of the Church. There is no shred of evidence to show that the English Church in the eleventh and twelfth centuries was governed by laws selected by itself.

PART II

THE RELATIONS OF ENGLAND WITH
THE PAPACY

CHAPTER VIII

LANFRANC

IT was necessary to be quite sure, in the first place, as to the law of the English Church. With our knowledge of that secure, we obtain a clearer perception of the whole situation and a key to the changes that ensued. We are concerned here, not with the ultimate issue between the *sacerdotium* and the *regnum* —which was to be the master of the other—for this does not concern English history at this time; but with the more immediate issue, arising in every country— —which was to be the master of the ecclesiastical officials. It might seem obvious that, if the Pope was acknowledged to be Head of the Church, he had the first claim to their obedience. But this was not so obvious to a generation brought up in the contrary tradition, and accustomed to the idea that obedience was due to the ruler ordained of God. In a contest of two powers for their allegiance, the bishops and their subordinates had ultimately a deciding voice; the law of the Church was bound to weigh heavily in their decision, so that it was all-important to discover what actually was the law to which they adhered.

While the attitudes of both Pope and king were clear and consistent throughout, the attitude of the bishops soon became clouded and confused. At first, indeed, they were whole-heartedly on the side of the king. They adopted the traditional standpoint, and they supported him both from conviction and from motives

of interest. But gradually the study of the law began
to have its effect, and then they were in a difficult
position. They were bound by it to obey the Pope;
they were pledged by their oath to the king, and
bound often by their fears and self-interest, and also
they were still convinced of their duty to God's
anointed. Hence they were in a serious dilemma, in
which they were sometimes relieved, sometimes still
further embarrassed, by other factors, such as the
changing fortunes of the contest of Empire and
Papacy, the political situation and its effect on the
power of the king, and the use, whether arbitrary or
otherwise, that the king made of his authority over
them. The story is a complicated one, but on the whole
the process of change, once it has begun under the
influence of the law upon ecclesiastical opinion, is
fairly constantly in one direction. We start with the
older tradition, and inevitably again with Lanfranc,
for it was he that set the tune to which in his day all the
other bishops danced.

The best general estimate of Lanfranc that I know
is contained in Heinrich Böhmer's *Die Fälschungen
Erzbischof Lanfranks von Canterbury*; though Böhmer
is convinced of Lanfranc's lack of scruple, he starts by
paying a fine tribute to his essential greatness. In
particular, he lays stress on the versatility with which
he could assume a new rôle, and his amazing efficiency
and prompt mastery of detail in whatever he undertook. This is undoubtedly true. He was, in the first
place, a famous teacher of the Civil Law at Pavia. As
a monk at Bec, he became a famous teacher of the arts

and of theology. He was versed in the various subjects of the normal curriculum, including Latin literature; but particularly did he read widely in the Bible and the Early Fathers, and became, for his day, an expert theologian. He wrote a commentary on the Pauline Epistles, and was welcomed by the Papacy as the great champion of orthodoxy against Berengar. Then, after a short spell as abbot at Caen, he was appointed archbishop, and threw himself whole-heartedly into his new task. For this one of the first requisites was a thorough knowledge of ecclesiastical law. He had evinced some familiarity with it before, but only of a general kind; and naturally his training in civil law made it easier for him to become an adept in canon law. The picture which I conjured up before from the evidence afforded by the Trinity College manuscript seems to me to fit exactly into its place here: the picture, I mean, of Lanfranc sitting down to the task with a Norman clerk beside him, working through the papal decrees and the canons of Councils in the book he had specially bought from Bec, and noting for future reference those passages which provided authority for the various sides of his work as metropolitan and primate. One cannot but admire the speed with which he gets up his brief, the mastery he obtains of all the details connected with his new position, and the thoroughness with which he carries out his novel duties.

He familiarises himself not only with the law but also with local customs and conditions, and he at once institutes a reorganisation of the English Church to bring it into line with the normal standards of the

Church as a whole. It is fair to believe that it was as a means to this end, and not merely from motives of personal ambition, that he asserted so resolutely his claim to be primate; for otherwise he would have been master only in his own province, and it was necessary to carry out the reconstruction in England as a whole, continuing and completing the work begun by the papal legates, whose sphere had been the whole kingdom. For the same reason he stoutly maintained the English custom of monastic cathedrals, where they existed, and with papal assistance prevented the introduction of secular canons at Canterbury and Winchester; from the secular clergy in England, married men for the most part, it was not possible to expect much assistance in promoting the new rules of ecclesiastical discipline. To the monastery of his own cathedral church, Christ Church, Canterbury, he gave a written constitution, which was based primarily on the Customs of Cluny. This he may have intended to become a uniform rule; it was certainly imitated elsewhere, as at St Albans, and manuscripts of it are not uncommon. His obvious qualities as an administrator caused William I to employ him in the secular government as justiciar during his own absence in Normandy, and here again Lanfranc fulfilled his duties with remarkable efficiency. The older he got, the more work he undertook, and yet with all these responsibilities there is no diminution of his amazing energy, no sign, until after the death of William I, that his activity was impaired by the burden of his years.

But, as an offset to this, was he, as Böhmer believes,

thoroughly unscrupulous, and prepared to adopt any means to achieve his end? Böhmer, I think, has conclusively shown that the papal letters quoted by Eadmer and others in support of the Canterbury claims were in part or in whole forgeries. But, while admiring his ingenuity and recognising the weight of some of his arguments, I do not feel that he has made out his case against Lanfranc. And as to the whole picture that he has sketched—of Lanfranc hurrying down to Canterbury after the Easter Council at Winchester, searching out papal documents, altering some to suit his purpose and using others as a model by which to compose forged documents of his own, doing this secretly by himself because he dared not employ a clerk who might expose the fraud, destroying the originals lest they should be used against him, and getting all this done so expeditiously that after the lapse of only seven weeks he could arrive triumphantly at the Whitsun Council at Windsor with his ten papal letters neatly written out to support his claim—this picture, taken as a whole, seems to me entirely fantastic. It is incredible that a stranger to England, to English history, and to English documents could have got up his brief and composed his documents in so short a space of time. But it is even harder to believe that he would, or could, have worked on his own. How could he have kept his doings to himself, and avoided the curiosity of the monks? And how could he have hoped to keep all this secret from them, since they must have known that the documents never existed before?

This does not by itself invalidate Böhmer's main

point, but the evidence throughout seems to me to be similarly strained in order to fit the thesis; especially am I confident that the manuscript evidence, which I have carefully examined, cannot bear the interpretation he has put upon it. However, it would be out of place for me here to attempt a critical treatment of this difficult question, though I hope to have the opportunity of doing so elsewhere.[1] I must content myself with stating my own view of what actually occurred. The point from which I start is Lanfranc's letter to Alexander II detailing the documents brought before the Council in support of his claim. He says: "prolata sunt antecessorum vestrorum Gregorii, Bonefacii, Honorii, Vitaliani, Sergii, item Gregorii, Leonis, item ultimi Leonis privilegia atque scripta". Except for the first and last of these, the list exactly corresponds with the authors of the first eight of the ten documents quoted by Eadmer. It is difficult to escape the conclusion that Lanfranc produced the first eight of Eadmer's documents.[2]

---

[1] Dr A. J. Macdonald (*Lanfranc*, Appendix 1; and more recently in Journal of Theol. Studies, vol. XXXII, pp. 39–55) has attempted to shift the blame from Lanfranc to Eadmer. I cannot agree with his final conclusion, but he has certainly made some good points against Böhmer, especially with regard to privilege 1; and he has fully exposed the weakness of Böhmer's arguments based on the phraseology of the forgeries and erasures in manuscripts.

[2] Eadmer has eight letters of the six Popes, two each from Boniface and Sergius. Much of Dr Macdonald's thesis depends on an unwarrantable assumption that Lanfranc had only one letter of each of the Popes he mentions. He urges that Lanfranc would have prefaced a second letter of Boniface or Sergius with the word *item*. But his use of *item* (before Gregory and Leo) is to distinguish a Pope from another of the same name previously mentioned. Dr Macdonald's further argument that Lanfranc had genuine documents from which Eadmer elaborated his forgeries afterwards I find

This does not mean that Lanfranc forged them himself or even knew them to be forged. Let us consider the common sense of the situation. It is surely certain that the first thing he would do when confronted by opposition to his claim to be primate would be to turn to the monks of Canterbury to prepare his brief for him, since he must have been unfamiliar himself with the past history and the evidence; and especially he would order a search to be instituted for papal privileges in support of his claim. He would not need to forge if there were genuine privileges in existence; but if he had enquired and found there were none, how could he have hoped to keep the fact of his forgery secret? I believe the monks prepared for him the case which he elaborated so successfully before the Council and which he described at length in his letter to the Pope—the evidence from Bede, the previous councils held by his predecessors, the professions of obedience made to them, and finally, "ultimum quasi robur totiusque causae firmamentum", the papal privileges, which were limited in number because, as his monks doubtless told him, the originals and copies of others had all been destroyed in the fire at Canterbury four years previously. The monks had both the time and the knowledge, which were lacking to him, to elaborate this most successful collection of evidence. It must be remembered, too, that the monks of Christ Church

difficult to believe. The documents were produced in full Council. If they clearly proved the case, what need was there for the later forgeries? And how in these circumstances could the subsequent fraud have escaped notice?

always showed themselves as zealous for the privileges
of Canterbury as their archbishop was; in the same
way that the canons of York showed an even greater
zeal than their archbishop on the other side, and sometimes had difficulty in stimulating him into asserting
his independence. The quarrel was as much one between the two chapters as between the two archbishops. Moreover, the Canterbury monks were certainly in possession of other forged documents; there
are certain forged canons giving privileges to monks
which turn up again and again on Canterbury manuscripts. And this helps to explain the peculiarity of
privilege 1, which has nothing to do with the primacy
but only enjoins that the chapter at Canterbury shall
always be monastic; it is most unlikely that Lanfranc
would have concocted it himself for this Council. It
was a point vital to the monks, and I suggest that they
took the opportunity of getting it established by
attaching this document to the evidence on behalf of
the primacy. The one or two[1] documents in Eadmer
which are not mentioned by Lanfranc were doubtless
concocted by the monks later on, probably when the

---

[1] I think it quite possible that Lanfranc actually had nine of the
ten documents given in Eadmer. In the manuscript text, printed by
Böhmer, no. 8, "Epistola Leonis papae...", is followed by "Memor-
abile factum", which concerns Pope Formosus, and this by no. 9,
"Idem omnibus episcopis...". The *idem* refers to Formosus, but
supposing that Lanfranc's copies also had these titles attached to
them, and that he quoted his list of Popes from the titles, he might
have passed over no. 9 as a second letter from Leo. This could only
be the case if he were not the forger. There is evidence that nos. 1–9
hang together, and that no. 10 is a later addition. It is not included
in the earliest text (B.M. Cotton Claudius A. iii and Faustina B. vi)
or in the Durham MS. (B. IV. 18), which contains the other nine and
was clearly written at Christ Church.

question became acute again in the first half of the twelfth century.

There is no question that the forgeries were done at Canterbury, and I think there can be little doubt that it was the monks who composed them. This still leaves it possible that Lanfranc was privy to the forgery, though I see no reason why he should have been. His part was only to present the case so cleverly prepared for him, and he obtained his verdict; the archbishop of York had to confess that he had no idea of the weight of authority on the Canterbury side. Nobody else suspected the forgery, and there is no reason why Lanfranc should have done so; the monks were not likely to tell him, and he could not have detected it by himself. Only one of the trained clerks of the papal chancery could have recognised where the forger went wrong.[1] Lanfranc had not the requisite knowledge; in this, at least, those who believe Lanfranc to be the forger must agree with me.

I think it would be possible to palliate the offence of the monks on the usual grounds that forgeries of this kind were made not in order to create a right but in order to avoid losing a right; that documents were so hard to preserve amid the perils of war and the dangers of fire, and that it is not unlikely that some of the monks remembered documents lost in the fire four years previously. But this defence would not exculpate Lanfranc; he could not defend forgery on that score, and, as Böhmer has pointed out, his training in

---

[1] Probably the forgery would have been detected at Rome, but I do not think the documents were sent to the Pope by Lanfranc. See below, p. 172, n. 1.

civil law must have given him a conviction of the heinousness of the offence. Therefore, if he was the forger we must admit that he was utterly unscrupulous. This does not fit with what we know of him and his associates and the general esteem in which he was held. A trait of that kind would not have escaped the notice of an able pupil, and that was the relation in which Alexander II had stood to him. It would not have escaped the notice of William I, who chose him for his great qualities and who would have regarded such a trait as a definite disqualification for his confidence. Above all, it would not have escaped the notice of St Anselm. Anselm was a saint whom it was not easy to deceive; he showed great perspicacity in reading the minds of the men whom he knew. His affection and esteem for Lanfranc are abundantly manifest in his correspondence; though Lanfranc's way was not always his way, he obviously had no doubt of his sincerity and honesty. I rate the unanimity of contemporary testimony to his high character above the hypotheses, for such they are and they are very insecurely based, of his modern traducer.[1] The picture that I have set over against Böhmer's is to my mind the only one that will fit all the facts.

The question of the forgery is not merely one of antiquarian interest. It colours our whole view of the man and the part he played, and of his attitude to authority in general. Certainly in his attitude to the

[1] Böhmer became so obsessed with his theory that he tried to prove that Lanfranc was consistently dishonest throughout his career. Dr Macdonald (J.T.S. p. 54) has exposed the weakness of some of his charges.

Papacy I feel that he was perfectly genuine, though
the Papacy doubtless appeared to him in different
lights at the various stages of his career. His early life
in Italy coincided with the deepest degradation of the
Papacy, when it was of no account save as an occasion
for gossip. He had already passed through the first
stage of his career—that of civil lawyer—and passed
into the second, of teacher and theologian, before the
Papacy was reformed. In this stage he was in close
touch with it. As monk and abbot he visited Rome
three times, first in 1050 when he not only vindicated
his own orthodoxy but also became the champion of
orthodoxy against Berengar; a second time in 1059 as
advocate for William I in the matter of his marriage
with Matilda, when he witnessed the recantation of
Berengar; and again as William's advocate in 1067
when he obtained permission for the translation of
bishop John of Avranches to the archbishopric of
Rouen. Basking in the sun of papal favour, he might
be inclined to exalt papal authority. From Nicholas
II, and from his former pupil Alexander II, he received letters of a most flattering nature, and these
letters, together with the decrees he had heard at the
great Council of 1059, are found written into his book
of ecclesiastical law. Once again he went to Rome, in
1071, the year after he became archbishop, both to
obtain the pallium and to plead the cause of the
primacy of Canterbury; and the singular favour of
Alexander II was shown by the conferring on him of
a second pallium, a rare mark of distinction. After
that date his personal contact with Rome ceased. The
death of Pope Alexander II in 1073 made a difference,

and so did his new rôle. Hitherto, as theologian, papal authority had magnified his importance; now, as archbishop, the great ecclesiastical administrator of a kingdom, it might be irksome.

Moreover, hitherto in his connection with the Papacy there had been no manifestation of papal authority that any reforming ecclesiastic of the early eleventh century would have regarded as at all unusual. The causes on which he came to Rome had been major issues which it was quite normal to refer to the Pope. He recognised the Pope as the source of law, quoting papal decretals, and relying on papal privileges to justify his claim to the primacy. The stringent papal decrees, especially against simony and clerical marriage, which he had heard in 1059, he added to his collection of papal decretals; and still, as archbishop, they would seem to him essential for the proper administration of the Church. That in the Council of Winchester (1076) he relaxed the decrees against clerical marriage is often quoted as a sign of his disobedience to papal decrees; but the fact that he allowed the parish clergy who were actually married to retain their wives was only an obvious recognition of existing conditions. The Popes themselves found it necessary to make exceptions in the case of England. Paschal II in 1107 gave a dispensation to Anselm to allow the sons of priests to hold benefices, so much was this the custom in England even then[1]; and Alexander III's decretals some seventy years later grant similar dispensations. Lanfranc was genuinely at one with the Papacy about reform.

[1] Eadmer, *Historia Novorum*, ed. Rule, M., Rolls Series, p. 185.

In all this he acts in accordance with custom and tradition. But it lay outside the range of his experience that a Pope should interfere with the normal course of episcopal government, especially with an archbishop in his province. No such thing had been heard of in Normandy, and given a zealous archbishop there seemed no occasion for it to happen. But after the accession of Gregory VII it became clear that the Pope regarded this as one of his normal functions. Lanfranc was entirely at one with William I on this issue; it is impossible to separate them in considering the policy henceforward adopted in the English Church. He was certainly not actuated by fear of the king, as Gregory VII suggested. If he had felt as Anselm did, he would have been equally fearless in withstanding the king, just as he withstood him when he was prior of Bec; it was his fearlessness as well as his capacity that made him so much the man after William's heart. Because he was so completely in accord with William's views he worked in harmony with William, who for the same reason could entrust to him the government of the Church in England. It involved a recognition of royal control, but this probably did not conflict with his views, for it had long been traditional on the Continent; it did not interfere with his work as archbishop; and it did provide just the barrier that he needed to protect him from the dangerous interference of the Papacy.

It was the more dangerous because, as he knew, it was justified by the strict letter of the law. With the pseudo-Isidorian decretals in front of him, he must have been aware of that. There he must have seen the numerous authorities that the Pope could quote to justify his interference, but he passed lightly over them and only marked one passage which upheld the right of anyone to appeal to the Pope. In the cases of Odo of Bayeux and William of Durham he did not deny the right of ecclesiastics to appeal to the Pope; he insisted, however, that it was not as ecclesiastics, but on secular grounds, that they had been condemned. There is an instance, too, in one of his letters (no. 31) of his dealing with a case that had gone on appeal to Rome and been referred to him by the Pope. On the other hand, there is no evidence that anyone who liked did or could appeal to Rome; it might be lawful, but it was certainly not traditional. And this is probably the distinction that Lanfranc drew between cases where obedience to the Pope was necessary and where it could justifiably be evaded. He is careful in his letters to the Pope to admit the full papal competence; but he had his own views about the extent to which that competence ought to be pushed. His methods are interesting to observe. In one instance, the case of bishop Herfast of Thetford and the abbey of St Edmund at Bury, he took action as the Pope instructed him to do, but not in the way the Pope intended. For, while Gregory wrote furiously about the insolence of Herfast in interfering in a monastery which had been put under the direct protection of the apostolic see,[1] Lanfranc contented himself with ordering the bishop in one letter (no. 22) to refrain from any action until he has come himself to hear both sides, and in another (no. 26) to refrain from making any claim

[1] Gregory VII, Reg. I, 31.

upon the abbey unless he can prove that the claim was maintained by his predecessors. He stresses in this letter the bishop's duty of obedience to himself as metropolitan, and quotes the authorities for this from canon law; he says not a word about the abbey being exempt from episcopal control and under papal protection.[1] This is a very instructive case. Lanfranc was a keen supporter of monasticism, but not to the extent of allowing monasteries to be exempt from episcopal control; as he showed later in his harsh treatment of the monastery of St Augustine at Canterbury.

Furthermore, while maintaining his own standpoint, he managed to avoid a conflict. On only one point did he meet with papal censure, and that was because of his non-compliance with Gregory's repeated orders to him to visit the apostolic see. So far as we know, he refrained from replying to Gregory on this point; perhaps he shielded himself behind the king's refusal, as he did on another important issue: "The verbal message brought by your legate, as best I could, I suggested to my lord the king, I advised him, but I could not persuade him. He will tell you in his own words why he could not give assent to your wishes" (no. 11). The concert between William and Lanfranc was, indeed, so close that their separate rôles are really indistinguishable. It will be convenient, then, at this point to consider them together in estimating the attitude towards the Papacy adopted by William I.

[1] Eadmer (*Historia Novorum*, ed. Rule, M., Rolls Series, pp. 132–133) says that Lanfranc indignantly took away from abbot Baldwin the privilege of exemption which he had received from Alexander II, and refused to return it. This sounds a very high-handed proceeding. More probably he refused to allow the abbot to use his privilege.

CHAPTER IX

WILLIAM THE CONQUEROR. THE TRADITIONAL OUTLOOK

I HAVE already suggested that William the Conqueror, as duke of Normandy, was exactly at the old standpoint of Henry II and Henry III, according to which the ruler was the instigator of reform and at the same time the master of the Church in his dominions. It is important to realise the significance of this. It explains both the cordial relations which William so long maintained with the Pope, for they were working for the same end, and also the ultimate disagreement, because they disagreed as to the means by which this end was to be attained. It enables us therefore to appreciate, almost to anticipate, his attitude to the Papacy throughout; and, further, to realise that, without any idea of a national Church, in fact without any idea of departing from the traditional practice of the universal Church, the view of papal authority that was current in Rome, and was penetrating into France and even into parts of Germany, could be disregarded in England and the Pope's orders calmly disobeyed. William I was behaving in the way that enlightened and spiritually-minded rulers had always behaved hitherto. The idea of a centralised Church directly controlled in all its parts by the Pope was novel to him, and therefore untenable; it involved a breach of tradition and custom, quite apart from the menace to his own authority. It was from every point of view distasteful to him, as it was to his contemporaries, Henry IV of Germany and Philip I of France; and it was put forward by a Papacy itself only recently reformed, whereas the dukes of Normandy had long been distinguished as reformers.

This does not mean that he repudiated papal authority in the Church. Far from it. He was naturally devout and, like his fellow-countrymen in South Italy, filled with deep regard for the papal office, a regard he was always careful to show. As everybody else, even in the first half of the eleventh century, he recognised the papal headship of the Church. I suggested before that there was an analogy with the position of the king in France, and I think that is very much how it may have appeared to William. The Pope has a unique position as the Head of the Church. He is the source of authority: so archbishops have to receive their pallia from him, and make to him their professions of faith; he, as it were, confirms them in their office. Refusal to confirm would have been another matter, and one that William did not contemplate; papal confirmation was a necessary formality, but no more. The Pope was also the exponent of the law of the Church, the authority who could be consulted in cases of doubt. His tribunal was the highest ecclesiastical tribunal, and so when issues arose between great officials—archbishops or bishops —recourse could and often must be had to Rome; just as tenants-in-chief of the king of France might in dispute with one another have recourse to the king, whom normally they would ignore. All important questions, then, beyond the normal competence of the local ecclesiastical courts would naturally be referred to the Pope. But that the Pope should of his own initiative interfere, and interfere in such a way as to limit the king's authority over any of his subjects, must obviously be prevented at all costs. This was the normal position of a tenth- or eleventh-century ruler.

So, then, he is guided in his dealings with the Church, not by the arbitrary caprices of a despot,[1] but by what appeared to him to be the commonplaces of the situation, dictated by necessity, by Norman tradition and custom, and by his conception of the kingly office. If we consider the details, I think it will appear that William's actions were throughout entirely natural and regularly consistent. He had already had contact with the Papacy when he was duke of Normandy. Firstly, there had been friction over his marriage with Matilda. Pope Leo IX had forbidden it at the Council of Rheims, but William, in defiance of the papal prohibition, married Matilda when the Pope was a prisoner of the Normans in South Italy; in 1059, however, he obtained papal recognition of the marriage in return for the performance of a penance—throughout, a typically Norman proceeding. There was also nothing out of the common in his reference to Rome in 1067 for the translation of a bishop. More noteworthy was his appeal for papal support for his invasion of England, but

---

[1] Too much stress must not be laid on the well-known passage in Eadmer (*Historia Novorum*, ed. Rule, M., Rolls Series, p. 9) beginning: "Cuncta ergo divina simul et humana eius nutum expectabant", which implies a despotic use of his power. Eadmer was the faithful companion in exile of Anselm, and he looked at this question of authority in the Church through Anselm's eyes, and with the vivid memory of William II's tyranny.

again, as he was careful to admit no claim arising from it, not an exception to his general policy. For he was particularly careful to stress that he was claiming his rightful inheritance, and not conquering another's; the charge of perjury against Harold brought the matter into the ecclesiastical courts, and it was natural, if not necessary, to refer a case of this magnitude to the supreme ecclesiastical court. It was important for him that he should be free from the charge of being a usurper. At Rome he gained the powerful support of the archdeacon, Hildebrand. It was entirely in keeping with Hildebrand's views that the Papacy should interfere on a moral issue; there was also the laudable, and to him almost irresistible, inducement that William's victory would mean the introduction of reform into the English Church and also the restoration of unity, for archbishop Stigand was a schismatic who had received his pallium from an anti-Pope and refused obedience to the lawful Pope. The result fully justified these expectations.

The Conquest achieved, the Conqueror still had pressing need of papal assistance. The radical re-organisation of the English Church was essential, including such drastic changes in the personnel that papal sanction was necessary to make them legal. The three legates sent by the Pope, at the synods of Win-chester and Windsor at Easter and Whitsun 1070, did William the service of disposing of certain English bishops and abbots, and promoting the foreigners chosen by him to replace them; especially did the deposition of Stigand make the way clear for Lan-franc, whose appointment was as acceptable to the

Pope as it was to the king. Then the period of urgency was over; Lanfranc and his subordinates could manage by themselves. Papal assistance was no longer required, and might indeed lead to papal interference, which must be prevented at all costs; in this, as in the whole of their ecclesiastical policy, William and Lanfranc were absolutely in accord.

William was, in fact, determined to be master of all his subjects; a dual authority in the kingdom was to him unthinkable. He was careful, as Eadmer remarks, to preserve the Norman practice—a practice common to all kingdoms—of appointing bishops and important abbots, and ensuring their obedience to himself. He could leave much of the ecclesiastical organisation in Lanfranc's hands, because Lanfranc was his man, and so were all the bishops; it was essential that they should not become the men of the Pope as well. He was not in this trying to create a national and independent Church. On the contrary, he had brought the English Church out of its backwater into the regular current once more. He made it an integral part of the Church, to be governed by the laws of the Church; as one of the first steps, the ecclesiastical courts, as in Normandy, were separated from the secular, and in them cases were to be heard in accordance with the "canones et episcopales leges"— the laws of the Church and the decrees of the bishops in Council. Local ecclesiastical councils had always been a feature of Church government, and they were accordingly re-instituted in England; as ruler William had a control and a veto over their legislation, but this was no novelty. They were not, however, as was usual

elsewhere, provincial councils, but, owing to Lanfranc's position as primate, councils of the whole
English Church, and this provided a desirable uniformity. Also the legislation they passed was not new,
or counter to Church law; it was based on the laws of
the Church. Naturally William recognised the papal
headship in England as he had in Normandy, allowing
it the degree of authority to which he had been
accustomed, and no more. Everything that was traditional and customary was to be maintained. So Lanfranc must receive his pallium from the Pope; but it
was now the rule at Rome that archbishops must
come to Rome to receive it. To this novelty William
submitted, and Lanfranc was probably not averse to
going; for the question of the primacy of Canterbury
had to be referred to Rome, and he hoped by his
personal advocacy to obtain papal assent.

But there must be no other novelties. So William
was careful to prevent any contact with the Papacy
that had not his express sanction. Nothing was to
come from Rome without his consent: Eadmer says
that he would not allow anyone to receive letters from
the Pope which had not first been shown to himself.
And, similarly, no one was to go to Rome without
leave, and probably then it would only be as William's
ambassador. Gregory VII wrote[1] indignantly in 1079
that "no king, not even a pagan king, has presumed
to act against the apostolic see in the way that William
unblushingly has acted; no one has been so irreverent
and insolent as to prevent bishops and archbishops
from coming to the threshold of the apostles". He

[1] Reg. VII, I.

was particularly urgent that Lanfranc, who had not been to Rome during his papacy, should come, and was much offended at his non-appearance. But William was deaf to the Pope's appeals. If bishops went to Rome they would come under papal control, and perhaps return with decrees that might be dangerous to royal authority. The safest course was to prevent them from going, and to prevent orders from Rome being admitted into the country without his permission. So a definite barrier was interposed. Any legate that came from Rome would be admitted only as an envoy to the king, not as a plenipotentiary with authority over the English Church. The decrees against lay investiture did not enter England until Anselm went to Rome and brought them back with him; the primate and his colleagues saw to the whole government of the Church; the ecclesiastical courts were adequate for the conduct of ecclesiastical cases in England.

From William's point of view the necessity of this barrier must have become apparent when the pupil and admirer of Lanfranc, Pope Alexander II, was succeeded by Gregory VII, whose fiery zeal and masterful energy were in direct contrast with the rather commonplace qualities of his predecessor. Gregory, for his part, had the highest hopes of William, for was he not the one prince who was promoting in his kingdom the thing that lay nearest to Gregory's heart, the reform and regeneration of the Church? But while he could speak of William as unique among all the lay rulers of his time in this respect, he was both mystified and indignant at the barrier interposed by William to prevent what he himself considered to be the normal activities of the Church, especially as this barrier did not elsewhere confront him. William, on his side, was anxious to be on good terms with the Head of the Church, who as cardinal had ardently supported his conquest of England. But he must have viewed with suspicion and dislike the action of the Pope against the ruler of Germany, and he doubtless noticed the gradual papal penetration of the French kingdom by permanent papal legates, which continued until it even invaded his own duchy of Normandy.

The climax came in 1079, when matters almost reached a crisis. The appointment of the archbishop of Lyons as primate over the four provinces of Lyons, Tours, Sens, and Rouen was as objectionable to the duke of Normandy as it was to the king of France. Further, the Pope raised objections to the appointment of William Bona Anima as archbishop, and deposed both bishop and abbot of Le Mans. He also gave instructions to his legate that at least two bishops from each province in England and Normandy were to attend the Lenten synod at Rome in 1080. William's attitude was again characteristic. The novelties, in the primacy of Lyons and the summons to Rome, he could ignore and cause his clergy to ignore; but the undoubted irregularities at Rouen and Le Mans were cases in which he, as a reformer, could not deny the papal competence. As previously in the case of his marriage, he sent an embassy to Rome and came to terms with the Pope, who recognised the archbishop of Rouen and, at William's special request, cancelled the deposition of the bishop of Le Mans and absolved the abbot. These incidents, however, doubtless stiffened William's determination with regard to England, and here his success was the more complete because it was so much easier to keep the English coasts immune from papal invasion.

It was at the supreme moment of Gregory VII's career, when he declared Henry IV of Germany deposed for ever and his rival Rudolf to be king in his stead, that he received the conciliatory embassy of William; it was a natural moment, then, for him to put forward his greatest claim with regard to England, which, if accepted, would have established papal authority in a decisive manner—the claim that William should do fealty to him for his kingdom. I wrote at length on this subject some years ago,[1] and in the main I abide by my former conclusions. I still believe that this demand of Gregory VII was brought as a verbal message by the legate Hubert with the letter of May 1080; this letter contains the famous simile of the sun and moon, and has other expressions in it which to contemporaries, I consider, would imply and were intended to imply a feudal subordination of king to Pope.[2] But on one point I was then very vague—the

[1] *Pope Gregory VII's demand for fealty from William the Conqueror* (Eng. Hist. Rev., vol. XXVI, pp. 225–238).

[2] This, I know, has not met with general acceptance. I am well aware that quotations such as that from Gelasius, and phrases such as "viventium possidere terram", have in themselves no feudal significance. But I still believe strongly that they were deliberately chosen; taken all together and in association with the general tone of the letter, I feel convinced as to how they would have struck the ear of a medieval ruler. Compare Adrian IV's use of "beneficium" in his letter to Frederick Barbarossa; the significance of this might have escaped us, if we had not got the Emperor's violent protest against it.

grounds on which Gregory based his claim—and I am sure now that I was wrong in suggesting that it was made by virtue of his spiritual authority, and therefore different from his claims in Spain and elsewhere. For I overlooked one very important piece of evidence which seems to me decisive, the letter[1] which Alexander II had previously written to William I on the same subject, a letter of which Gregory VII must have been cognisant and in the composition of which he may have had some hand. Unfortunately we do not possess the whole letter, but only two fragments from it, and it is of interest to notice that they have survived only because they were quoted by Cardinal Deusdedit in his collection of canons, among a number of papal letters denoting territory subject to St Peter and the *census* payable therefrom—a sort of early "liber censuum". Deusdedit is quoting Alexander II's letter as proof of England's subordination to the Papacy and the consequent payment of *census*. In the first fragment the Pope says that the English kingdom, from the time of the introduction of Christianity, was "sub apostolorum principis manu et tutela", until some sons of Satan rejected God's covenant and led the English people from the way of truth. In the second fragment he says that while the English were faithful (*fideles*) they showed their devotion by making an annual payment to the apostolic see, part of which went to the Pope, part to the *schola Anglorum*. Alexander II is clearly linking up the old allegiance with the payment to Rome, and it can hardly be doubted that in the middle portion of the letter, not

[1] Migne, PL. CXLVI, col. 1413.

quoted by Deusdedit, he urged the return of England to its old allegiance.

I do not doubt that Deusdedit's attribution of this letter to Alexander II is correct; he was writing at the end of Gregory VII's Papacy and could consult the registers, and his other attributions on this topic of subjection to Rome are correct. So we possess only Alexander II's letter to William and William's reply to Gregory VII. But, as I have said, I believe that Gregory's demand came in the form of a verbal message brought by the legate Hubert, and is therefore irrecoverable. However, I think Alexander's letter helps us to reconstruct the message which Gregory gave to his legate. Firstly, I presume that he referred, like Alexander, to the early subordination of England to Rome and its subsequent lapse; this is similar to what he said about Spain.[1] Secondly, he possibly referred to the papal support given to William's conquest, which he had already alluded to, especially emphasising the part played by himself, in his letter to William in the previous month; it is not unlikely that there was a similar reference in the missing portion of Alexander's letter. Thirdly, he doubtless referred, like Alexander, to the payment of Peter's Pence as evidence of the old allegiance of England. In fact, I think that Gregory's message must closely have followed the lines of Alexander's

---

[1] Reg. IV, 28. In the case of Spain the claim was probably based on the Donation of Constantine, which had come to the front again owing to the revival of the False Decretals, in which it appears. Was this also the basis of the claim on England? The conversion of England under Gregory I was often used to claim authority for the Roman over the English Church, but not over the English kingdom.

letter,[1] and, if so, the exact meaning of William's reply is made comprehensible. It is a curt reply; probably he had previously replied to Alexander II in less abrupt terms, and was annoyed at the claim being repeated. To the appeal to early history, he replies denying that his predecessors had ever done fealty; to the references to the Conquest, he replies that he made no promise himself of fealty; while he is very careful to dissociate the payment of Peter's Pence from any suggestion of it being a tribute to Rome. That this payment was so regarded by the Papacy is clear from the definite statements of later Popes, and from the reference to it in the *Liber Censuum*. So, then, I consider that Gregory VII based his claim to England, as to Hungary and elsewhere, on what he believed to be historical precedent, and in justification of his claim adduced as evidence the payment of Peter's Pence, for which indeed there was historical proof.[2]

At any rate he had to be content with the recognition of his lesser claim, without the implications that he drew from it. The resistance of William was too formidable, nor could he marshal his forces to break

[1] Denmark provides a closely parallel case. Deusdedit similarly quotes a letter of Alexander II claiming *census* from King Suein Estridson, and Gregory VII similarly recites what took place in Alexander's papacy (Reg. II, 75).

[2] Professor Fliche (*La Réforme Grégorienne*, vol. II, pp. 345 foll.) tries to make out that Gregory VII never made the claim at all, but that it was made by his legates who exceeded their instructions. This unlikely hypothesis goes against all the evidence. Professor Fliche supports himself on Gregory's letter to Hubert blaming another legate, Teuzo, for abusing the English king. The fact that William mentions Hubert as the bearer of the message, and Gregory blames Teuzo for acting contrary to his orders, Professor Fliche considers as a divergence of detail that is of no importance.

it down now that his struggle with Henry IV was already recommencing. There were other considerations, too, to be taken into account. In 1081 he wrote[1] to his legates in France instructing them to remove the suspension they had laid upon the Norman bishops for their neglect to come to the synod to which they had been summoned. Nothing, he said, must be done to irritate William; one who above all other kings had forwarded the work of reform must be treated leniently, in spite of his failings in certain respects. In this spirit, while he spoke violently behind William's back about the imprisonment of bishop Odo of Bayeux, to his face he rebuked him in the gentlest of terms.[2]

William, then, had had his way. He had maintained the traditional and resisted the novel, in the government of the Church. But he can hardly have been without misgivings as to the future, and he seized the opportunity afforded to him by the appearance of a rival to Gregory VII in the person of Wibert of Ravenna, the anti-Pope Clement III. He did not, indeed, recognise Clement as Pope; he did not decide between the two Popes himself, nor did he allow any of his subjects to decide for themselves. This removed any question of papal authority at all. It could not be a permanent solution, but it was very satisfactory while it lasted, and equally so to Lanfranc as to William. Lanfranc rebuked a supporter of the anti-Pope, who had written violently denouncing Gregory

[1] Reg. IX, 5.
[2] Reg. IX, 37 to William. The other letter, written to archbishop Hugh of Lyons, is given as ep. coll. 44 in Jaffé's *Monumenta Gregoriana*, p. 570.

VII; England, he said, had not made up its mind. At the same time, he received three letters from the anti-Pope, all of which were entered in at the end of his book of ecclesiastical law, the manuscript now in Trinity College, Cambridge[1]; and the probability is that this was done at his direction, or at least with his cognisance. Probably both William and Lanfranc would have preferred the victory of a Pope who was subservient to a lay ruler, but at present they remained neutral, awaiting the issue, and William II followed suit. This was, perhaps, the one case in which William I could not have appealed to tradition in his favour, unless indeed he regarded his royal authority as having an imperial favour; in the attitude of William II, especially in the speech of bishop William of Durham on his behalf to Anselm,[2] there is more than a suggestion of this.

The key to William's attitude is tradition. He had no desire to introduce innovations; he was not attempting to create a national Church, nor, like Henry VIII, to abolish papal authority and make the king the supreme Head of the Church. He was following along the lines that were traditional not only in his own duchy but in Europe as a whole, and he was doing what kings and bishops elsewhere believed to be right. Henry IV of Germany precipitated the

---

[1] They have been edited from this MS. by F. Liebermann in Eng. Hist. Rev., vol. XVI, pp. 328–332. On the strength of these letters, P. Kehr (*Zur Geschichte Wiberts von Ravenna*, Sitzungs-berichte der preuss. Akad. der Wissenschaften, 1921, pp. 356 foll.) decides that England gave the anti-Pope a qualified recognition. This, I think, makes the position too definite.

[2] Eadmer, *Historia Novorum*, ed. Rule, M., Rolls Series, p. 60.

great struggle of Empire and Papacy in the attempt to recover the position his father Henry III had held in the Church, and had held without challenge; and in a smaller sphere Philip I of France was of the same mind but lacked the power to resist the papal advance. William was successful, and they failed. And his success was due mainly to three causes. Firstly, to the strength of his position as king. He was unquestioned master in England, whereas Philip was hopelessly weak in France and Henry IV was continually involved in civil war in Germany. Secondly, there seems to have been no thought in England of opposition to his ecclesiastical policy, no papalist party such as the other rulers had to contend with; on the contrary, he received whole-hearted support from the ecclesiastical officials with Lanfranc at their head. Thirdly, and most important of all, he was a sincere supporter of Church reform. Therefore, on the ecclesiastical side he was not open to attack where they were particularly vulnerable. It was the evils resulting from lay control—simony, secularisation of the episcopate, alienation of Church property—that led the Popes to attack lay control and to concentrate on their own independent and absolute control of the Church. William, owing to his zeal for reform, did not expose himself to these attacks, as his contemporaries on the Continent did; the Papacy was willing in his case to acquiesce in what it considered to be an irregular state of affairs, because the end for which it was working was being effectively promoted. His successors, however, did not follow him in this, and they sacrificed, accordingly, one of his chief assets.

CHAPTER X

ST ANSELM. THE RISE OF A PAPAL PARTY

THE first thing to be noted about Anselm is that he was a foreigner and came, like Lanfranc, from North Italy, though his native town of Aosta, close to the St Bernard passes, was far removed, geographically and politically, from Lanfranc's home at Pavia. It was actually within the territories of the count of Savoy, and therefore in a region more friendly to reform than the anti-papal Lombardy. But it is of more importance to remember that Anselm was born in 1033, a generation later than Lanfranc. Lanfranc had left Italy and was already at Bec before the Papacy had been reformed. Anselm left Italy nearly twenty years later than Lanfranc, and by that time the Papacy had already been reformed, and Leo IX by his journeyings and holding of synods had made North Italy, France, and Germany familiar with the Pope and with papal authority. When, hardly yet of age, he left his home, it was first of all in Burgundy, where the reform movement was strong, that he stayed before he went north to Normandy; his travels, Eadmer states in his life of Anselm, lasted for three years in all. He was for a time at Bec as student and teacher before he decided to take the monastic vows; this he did in 1060, in his twenty-seventh year, the year after the great Lateran synod of Nicholas II which promulgated the Papal Election Decree, stringent reforming decrees especially against simony and clerical marriage, and the condemnation of Berengar's heresy; from

Lanfranc, who was present and kept a copy of the official proceedings, Anselm must have heard the fullest details. By 1060, then, the first chapter in his life was closed. He could have had no recollection of the unreformed Papacy; he saw it in the first vigour and enthusiasm of its regeneration and its recovered headship.

The next thirty-three years, the best years of his life, were spent in the monastery of Bec, three of them as simple monk, fifteen as prior, fifteen again as abbot. They are entirely devoted to monastic pursuits and to the production of the treatises for which he is famous. Of the world at large he seems hardly conscious. The numerous letters (considerably over one hundred) which have survived from his correspondence of those years contain practically no references even to ecclesiastical politics, with the notable exception of the letters that passed between him and Pope Urban II. He was not employed on great missions as Lanfranc had been. Reluctantly he had to go to England on the secular business of his monastery; normally, according to Eadmer, he delegated this to trusted monks, devoting himself to the contemplation of God, and to the instruction, the admonition, and the correction of his monks. As teacher and as master he was alike admirable. He was thoroughly human, understanding and making allowances for the difficulties and the temptations incidental to monastic life. Common sense, rather than a rigid application of rules, was the essence of his government, and on this he based his advice to others, by whom it was so often sought; a typical letter is the one in which he suggests to an abbot that he is spoiling his pupils by not sparing the rod. He could be severe, however, when personal and selfish ambition led a monk to a breach of the rule. He saw into the minds of men, sympathising with their weakness and exposing their faults; in later days he displayed a very accurate perception of the point of view of his antagonists.

It is tempting to dwell on St Anselm, one of the most attractive of all medieval churchmen, in this period of his happiness and real greatness. But I am only concerned here with noting his main characteristics, especially his absorption in the monastic and contemplative life, in order to mark his essential difference from Lanfranc, and therefore the entirely different outlook with which he undertook the duties of archbishop. Lanfranc was the man of action, anxious to achieve, ready for any responsibility. Anselm was the thinker, desirous to live the contemplative life, shunning responsibility. As it was the versatility of Lanfranc that was remarkable, so it was the single-mindedness of Anselm. He did not, like Lanfranc, put off the old when he donned the new rôle. If he had a legal training in Italy, he left there so young that he cannot have made much advance in it. He was above all a theologian, and his reading was most deep in the Bible and the Early Fathers. Some study of canon law he must have made, though his references to it are very few. In one letter (I. 56), written from Bec before he became abbot (i.e. before 1078), he quotes two decretals, both apocryphal, of Calixtus I and Gregory I; as they are quoted together by Burchard, it was probably from Burchard that he took them. After he had become archbishop, he quotes in one letter (III. 12) from the Fourth Council of Toledo, for which Burchard, Ivo, or Lanfranc's collection might be the source; in another (III. 159) he quotes a decretal at second-hand, and in this case the source is probably Ivo's *Pannormia*.[1] That is all that I have discovered, except that, like most of his contemporaries, he quotes from the letters of Gregory the Great; he also occasionally says that he has not time to look up the authorities. There is nothing to parallel the careful study of canon law made by Lanfranc in order to establish the legal support for his authority and his actions. On the contrary, he is much more concerned with papal authority than with his own, and admits obedience to that as his first duty. If he read through the False Decretals, this was the position to which they led him; and it would be typical of him to go to the law to find out what his duty was, not, as Lanfranc, in order to get from it what served his purpose and his position.

The crucial point is his acceptance of papal authority, of the reality of the papal headship of the Church. It was more natural that, as prior and abbot, he should hold this position, and he had been in correspondence not only with Urban II but also with archbishop Hugh of Lyons, the most advanced of papal legates. It was not in his nature to change when he became archbishop. He prefaces his work *De Fide Trinitatis* with a letter to Urban II, submitting it to the Pope's

---

[1] Anselm gives it as a decretal of Eugenius, as Ivo does in his *Pannormia*. In Burchard and in Ivo's *Decretum* it is attributed to Yginus.

judgment, because all questions of faith must be submitted to the Pope. He writes to Paschal II (IV. 2) that the direction and councils of the sons of the Church depend on the authority of the apostolic see. This is not merely the ordinary language of deference in addressing the Pope. He writes even more strongly to others. For instance, in two letters addressed to lay nobles (III. 65 and IV. 13), he speaks of the necessity of obedience to the decrees of the Pope; disobedience to the Pope is disobedience to St Peter (for the Pope is the vicar of St Peter), and therefore is disobedience to God. This is the language of Gregory VII himself; obedience to the Pope, as the representative of St Peter and so of God, Gregory claimed even from kings, and had written in this sense to William I in 1080. How much more certainly, then, was it due from an archbishop.

This it was that was the main issue between Anselm and William II, and the sole issue between him and Henry I. William II might be brutal and violent, a despoiler of churches and of Church property; questions of aids and services might cause friction between them; but the vital issue arose from Anselm's patient obedience to the law of the Church and William's stubborn determination to uphold the customs of his father. Anselm himself details the chief points at issue in a letter to archbishop Hugh of Lyons (III. 24), and again in a letter to Paschal II (III. 40) shortly after Urban II's death. He emphasises the fact that William in all the ways he mentions was acting contrary to the will and the law of God; they were all definitely breaches of ecclesiastical law. On some of these, the refusal of William II to allow the holding of Church councils and his appropriation of Church property, William I would have been in agreement with Anselm. But on the two most important points Anselm would have found William I as rigid as William II.

The first of these was the recognition of Urban II as Pope. This William I had insisted to be a matter for his own decision; in Anselm's view it could not be left to the judgment of a lay ruler. It was decided already by the law of the Church, by the Election Decree, so that there could be no doubt that Urban was lawful Pope, while Clement had been violently intruded by the Emperor. As abbot, he had accepted Urban as Pope, and had made it clear before his consecration that he recognised Urban; therefore no appeal to the " customs " of the country could weigh with him at all. It was his duty, besides, to pay the ceremonial visit to Rome to make his profession of faith and receive the pallium, and he complained to the archbishop of Lyons that, as a year had elapsed since his consecration without this duty having been fulfilled, his archiepiscopal rank was in danger. He could point, too, to the precedent of Lanfranc's visit to Rome for this purpose. Such a visit was the last thing William II wanted. He managed for the time to avert it, but only at the cost of having to recognise Urban II as Pope and to allow the entry of a papal legate, bearing the pallium, into his kingdom. So on the first issue Anselm was successful.

He was equally successful on the second point, his right to be allowed to visit Rome and to appeal to the

Pope. The mere request threw William into a rage, and Anselm had to face stronger opposition than before. At Rockingham he had been deserted by all the bishops, but the lay barons were sympathetic; on this occasion they as well as the bishops seem to have been shocked by his desire to violate custom and the king's prerogative. As far as the king was concerned, it was a crucial point, and William II recognised this as clearly as his father had done. But he made the tactical error of giving Anselm the alternative, either of doing satisfaction for his offence in making the request, and promising not to repeat it and not to appeal to the Pope; or of leaving the country at once. He doubtless intended the exile to be permanent. Anselm chose exile and forfeiture, and so got to Rome, and the result of this was immediately apparent on William II's death. It led to the quarrel with Henry I, which once more turned on obedience to the Pope and to papal decrees, obedience, that is to say, to the law of the Church that was current at Rome.

The barrier which William I had interposed to prevent papal intervention in England had hitherto been effective. It had kept papal decrees out of England, so that there had been no word there of opposition to lay investiture; even Anselm had raised no objection to being invested with ring and staff by William II nor to doing homage to him. It was equally important to keep English bishops from visiting Rome, lest they should learn obedience to the Pope and bring back the decrees with them. This policy was defeated by Anselm's return to England after his exile and residence in Rome. While he was there, Urban II held his last great synod at St Peter's, at which the leading decrees of his Papacy were promulgated anew; Eadmer, an eyewitness, especially mentions the decrees forbidding lay investiture and homage. His evidence is confirmed by Anselm himself, who repeatedly quotes from these two decrees in his letters, saying that he had heard them in the synod at Rome presided over by Urban II, and that he had therefore no alternative but to obey them.[1] It was owing to these decrees that he came at once into conflict with the new king, Henry I, who indeed was most anxious to welcome him back and receive his support, and who was greatly assisted by him in the matter of his marriage and on the occasion of his brother Robert's invasion of England. It was, therefore, a shock to him when Anselm at once refused to do him homage, or to have communion with any bishops or abbots who had received investiture from the king. The long drawn out negotiations, the second exile of Anselm, the final settlement of 1107, are all too familiar to need repetition here.[2] The king gave up investiture and Anselm in return promised not to withhold consecration from those who had done homage to the king. This was the concession allowed by Paschal II as a temporary expedient, until the king's mind should be softened. The royal control was little affected, because he treated the concession as a per-

---

[1] As far as the decree against investiture was concerned, Anselm had also heard it on an earlier occasion. Paschal II (Eadmer, *Historia Novorum*, p. 139) speaks of it as having been passed at the Council at Bari, where both he and Anselm were present.

[2] Dean Church's *St Anselm* still provides the best narrative account of these events.

manent one, and cleverly twisted it round so that he was able to insist on homage preceding consecration, while he was careful to control the actual appointments. In this, at any rate, the Constitutions of Clarendon faithfully repeat the customs of Henry I.

But for the third time Anselm had been successful. Once again he had insisted on obedience to the Pope and to papal decrees. The question at issue was not one on which he felt keenly himself, apparently, but the Pope had ordered, and until the Pope decreed otherwise he must obey the order. He stuck to his point and he carried it. This was, in fact, of greater importance than the other two cases, because it was so much more of a novelty. And the repeated victories of Anselm had their cumulative effect on the increase of papal authority in England. Not merely the old law, but the new decrees passed at Rome were enforced in England. It was the first breach made in the royal barrier, and it was never during the Middle Ages completely closed again.

Anselm in a sense stood by himself, in putting obedience to the Pope in the forefront of his duties as an ecclesiastic and at the same time in acting quite fearlessly in accordance with his convictions. It was this combination of courage and conviction that mattered. Nothing else could avail for the introduction of papal authority into England, since the king was determined to resist and had the power to do so; only by gaining support within the country could the Pope gain a footing there. So far there had been no sign of a papal party in England. Lanfranc, who

lacked neither courage nor conviction, had been whole-
heartedly on the side of the king, and the other bishops
showed no hesitation in following his lead. It may be
queried whether they acted thus through conviction,
or through lack of courage, or merely from self-
interest. Anyhow, it must be remembered that they
were chosen by William himself, and were therefore
men on whose obedience he felt he could rely. During
his reign there were in all eighteen appointments to
the fifteen English bishoprics.[1] Canterbury we can
leave out of account; Rochester, too, for being subject
to Canterbury the appointment to it seems to have
rested with Lanfranc, and he appointed in succession
two monks who had been under him at Bec and Caen.
At Worcester, the Englishman Wulfstan survived the
Conqueror, and so did another pre-Conquest bishop,
Giso of Wells, who had come from Lorraine. In the
remaining eleven bishoprics, fifteen appointments
were made by William I. Two of them came from
Lorraine, the others were all Normans, and eight of
them had previously been clerks of his chapel. It was
unlikely that from them would come any opposition
to royal authority in the Church. On the other hand,
they seem to have been suitable for their office, with
the exception of Herfast of Thetford, and zealous in
their duties. It is not necessary to assume that their
real views were prevented from expression by fear of
the king. They acted, I believe, conscientiously in
accepting the traditional; no other course had been

[1] Of the pre-Conquest bishops who were left in possession of
their sees, four were Englishmen, one a Norman, and three from
Lorraine.

put before them, and it needed a very exceptional man to take the initiative in such a matter.

There was, indeed, one ecclesiastic who not only accepted the royal control with conviction, but was also prepared to justify it to the fullest—the writer known, probably not very accurately, as "the Anonymous of York". He is, however, in many respects unique. There are some thirty tracts in all, attributed to one writer by Böhmer who has edited the majority of them,[1] and they are all contained in a unique manuscript which is in the library of Corpus Christi College, Cambridge, and apparently comes from Canterbury; how they managed to survive is a mystery. They form the only English contribution to the mass of pamphlet literature which was evoked by the contest of *sacerdotium* and *imperium*, and they display a more extreme standpoint than any of the pro-imperial tracts. The royal power is superior to the sacerdotal; it is of divine, the other of human nature. Christ was both king and priest, God and man: as king, equal to the Father as touching His Godhead; as priest, inferior to the Father as touching His manhood. Further, they seem almost to anticipate fourteenth-century attacks on the Papacy. They deny the Petrine theory, urging that no greater authority was given to St Peter than to the other apostles. Objection is raised not merely to the primacy of Lyons over Rouen, of Canterbury over York, but to the primacy of any church, even that of Rome, over any other. Each

---

[1] Partly in the Mon. Germ. Hist. *Libelli de lite*, vol. III, partly as an appendix to his *Kirche und Staat in England und in der Normandie im xi. und xii. Jahrhundert* (Leipzig, 1899).

bishop is the independent ruler of his diocese; the exemption of the monastery of Fécamp from the archbishop of Rouen is attacked on the ground that all exemptions are wrong. Canons and decrees should be obeyed, but not all are of equal validity. And, finally, there is a sturdy defence of clerical marriage and the ordination of the sons of priests.

These are a few of the striking points urged in this collection. Those that I have mentioned can, I think, possibly be attributed to the same writer; in many cases the same phrases are used. But not all the tracts are by the same hand; one or two express views quite contradictory to those I have mentioned. As to the author of the major portion of the collection, he is certainly anonymous. There are a few names of places mentioned, but no name of any contemporary personage, Pope, king, bishop, or anyone. He seems careful to keep his remarks in the abstract, and to avoid any concrete allusions to contemporaries. The allusions he makes to places prove him to be a subject of the English king. Böhmer has managed to work out an ingenious biography of him, the first part of which seems to me to be quite likely. The fact that he not only attacks the primacy of Lyons over Rouen, but also the exemption of the monastery of Fécamp from the jurisdiction of the archbishop of Rouen, does suggest that he was connected with the church of Rouen. Also his defence of clerical marriage and the ordination of priests' sons may be connected with the fact that archbishop William of Rouen (1079–1110) was the son of a priest. Clerical marriage was, indeed, still common in France as in England. Anselm in his

letters (II. 33) describes the persecution of the bishop
of Beauvais by his canons and clergy, because he tried
to get them to dismiss their wives. I think his Norman
origin, at any rate, is certain.

But I cannot agree with the further inference that,
because he supports York against Canterbury, therefore he must have gone to England and become a
canon of York. He had stated his objections to all
primacies in defending Rouen against Lyons; and, in
the early part of Henry I's reign, it would be a natural
thing for a supporter of royal authority to defend
York, since, owing to his difficulty with Anselm, the
king was temporarily on the side of York. He must at
least have visited England, and possibly he was at
Henry's coronation; he is able to detail the coronation
rite of the English kings in his most important tract—
"On the Consecration of bishops and kings"—which
is clearly a defence of Henry's right to appoint and invest bishops, though Henry is not mentioned. A
Norman, attached to the church of Rouen, might be
expected to be a stout supporter of Henry I. Possibly
he became a royal chaplain, and so visited and stayed
in England. Violent as he is against the papal claims,
he nevertheless quotes from the pseudo-Isidorian decretals in his defence of Rouen; while, in his pamphlet
on Consecration, he clearly has before him a copy of the
canons of Councils, and as he *inter alia* quotes at
length from the Council of Chalcedon, we are able to
observe that he was using a normal pseudo-Isidorian
collection, and not the collection introduced by Lanfranc, which was apparently the only one current in
England at this time.

Altogether it is a peculiar case. He seems to be so deliberately anonymous, for, though he does seem to have particular instances in view, he is very careful to avoid supporting a particular king or attacking a particular Pope. This looks like caution or fear, and it was doubtless justified; for in his generation he was a solitary and a unique figure. He went farther than even the kings would have cared to go. They did not deny the papal headship, and, except for William II, who showed no interest in the matter either way, they did deliberately attack clerical marriage. I do not think that he can be said to represent anyone but himself. His views were as extreme on the one side as were the papal on the other, and to neither would the normal bishop adhere. He remains therefore isolated. However, I think the normal English bishop at the beginning of the twelfth century would have inclined to his standpoint more readily than to Anselm's. They still believed it to be their duty to obey the royal commands, and Anselm's refusal to do so undoubtedly shocked many of them. Belief in the sacred character of the kingly office was not confined to this anonymous clerk; and it is a factor in the situation which is rather apt to be overlooked.

At any rate, in William I's reign it does seem probable that the bishops conscientiously supported both his reforming policy and his view of royal authority. As far as the abbots are concerned, their influence does not seem at present to have extended beyond their monasteries, and it is only occasionally that a regular was appointed as bishop; Canterbury and Rochester are exceptions, and William of St Carileph was an abbot before becoming bishop of Durham. A number of English abbots survived, three even into William II's reign, but new appointments were as a general rule made from Norman abbeys.[1] In these appointments Lanfranc clearly had a considerable share, and the result was that in many cases the monasteries were reformed, were well-regulated, and became centres of study; such I should judge to be true, for instance, of Christ Church Canterbury, St Albans, Gloucester, Westminster. Gradually their influence began to be felt outside, especially of those in which there was a study of ecclesiastical law; and again William II by deliberately leaving so many abbeys vacant for his own financial advantage would certainly tend to create among the regulars a feeling inimical to royal control. Furthermore, monastic exemptions were beginning, in spite of Lanfranc's hostility to them; the monasteries more and more tended to lean on Rome. Lanfranc himself, as abbot of Caen, had obtained a privilege for his monastery from Alexander II. On this point the abbots welcomed, and the bishops disliked, the authority of Rome.

It is not until the reign of William II that signs of dissent from royal control appear, and though the earliest instances are of regulars, it is as bishops that they take action. There is first of all the case of bishop William of Durham, on trial for treason before the Council, who disturbs his judges by appealing to the canon law. He claims, first, to be tried in the eccle-

---

[1] A valuable survey of *Abbatial elections*, 1066–1216, has been made by Dom David Knowles in Downside Review, vol. XLIX, pp. 252–278 (May 1931).

siastical courts; secondly, that his authority and possessions shall be restored to him before he is put on trial; and finally he appeals to the Pope, producing before the assembly his book of the "law Christian" as authority for his right to do so. I have already suggested that this book was probably the volume of *Decreta Pontificum* (now in Peterhouse library) which he presented to his cathedral library. If so, it was with a copy of Lanfranc's own collection that he faced him. Lanfranc, who had marked the passage in his own book, could not deny the right of a bishop to appeal; he could only deny that William of Durham was being tried as a bishop.

However, bishop William must not be regarded too seriously. He was taking a very unusual step, but only to evade judgment, not as a matter of principle. A few years later he is the spokesman against Anselm, shocked that Anselm dare recognise a Pope whom the king has not recognised. Yet he had himself appealed to a Pope whom the king had not recognised. A more genuine case is that of Herbert Losinga, monk of Fécamp and abbot of Ramsey, who paid money to the king when he was appointed bishop of Thetford. In 1093, smitten with remorse for his simony, he hurried off to Rome without leave, surrendered his bishopric to the Pope, and received it back with the papal absolution; and still Pope Urban II had not been recognised by William. The king was enraged, and took from Herbert his pastoral staff. But the bishop soon made his peace with the king, and later we find him acting as one of Henry I's representatives against Anselm on the investiture question.

These two cases, slight in themselves, are straws
showing that the wind was veering. The leaven of the
ecclesiastical law was beginning to work, and the king
could no longer rely on acquiescence with tradition.
Anselm's was a case of far greater magnitude, but if
he had remained in isolation he would have achieved
nothing. He soon found that he was not alone, and
that he had other adherents besides his faithful monks.
The bishops of Hereford and Salisbury, who with their
fellow-bishops had renounced obedience to Anselm
at Rockingham, were smitten with remorse, and
sought and obtained absolution from him. Of greater
significance, however, was it that, in his investiture
dispute with Henry I, two of the king's own nominees,
the bishops-elect of Winchester and Hereford, refused
to receive royal investiture and threw in their lot with
Anselm. So not merely had Anselm won his victories
for obedience to the Pope for himself; he had gained
adherents among the bishops. The barrier interposed
to prevent papal interference was firm against attacks
from outside; it could only be pierced from within.
It was a small breach that had been made, but there
was now the nucleus of a papal party in England, and
so papal authority, excluded by William I, had obtained a foothold which it was not to lose again until
the Reformation.

CHAPTER XI

HENRY I. THE MAINTENANCE OF ROYAL
CONTROL

WE have seen that the success of William I,
compared with the failure of his contemporaries (though their policy was the same
as his), was due to three main causes: to the strength
of his political position, to the absence of ecclesiastical
opposition within the country, and to his zeal for
reform in the Church, which made him so much less
vulnerable to attack on ecclesiastical grounds than
they were. This third advantage was immediately
thrown away by his successor. William II's rule of the
Church was purely selfish, in his own and not in its
interests. He cared nothing for reform, he appro-
priated Church property and left sees, and especially
abbeys, vacant; on the ecclesiastical side he became
immediately vulnerable. He was undoubtedly, from
his point of view, unfortunate in his archbishop, for
William I could not have tolerated Anselm's un-
questioning obedience to the Papacy. But Lanfranc
and William I could never have worked in harmony
had William been of the same temper as his son;
Lanfranc was no time-server as were so many of
William II's bishops. William II exposed himself, as
Philip I and Henry IV had done, to the criticism that
lay control meant the secularisation of the Church.
He antagonised all who were zealous for reform and
drove them into the papal camp; and he provided a
mark for the Papacy to shoot at. His father had been

doubly armed, morally as well as physically, but he himself had to rely on force to maintain his position. This, indeed, he was able to do, and he had a further advantage in that the Papacy could pay little heed to anything but its struggle with the Empire. Henry I, on the whole, followed in his father's footsteps, though rather from policy than from conviction, but a gap had been made in the defences, and England was no longer solid behind the king.

For these reasons, then, the history of the twelfth century was to be very different from the history of the eleventh. In William II's reign the royal control had been identified with spoliation of the Church, and henceforward it was suspect in spite of William I. Moreover, the Popes were no longer inclined to condone lay control because it advanced reform, and the kings of England, if they did not openly imitate William II, had none of William I's zeal for reform. Otherwise they imitated his policy; all of them referred to the "customs" which he had instituted, and tried their best to enforce them. But these could only be maintained if the political authority of the king was adequate. There is, accordingly, a striking change during the reign of Stephen, and the Papacy begins to assert itself as it had done in France in the eleventh century, when the French monarchy was weak. Similarly it was political weakness that was responsible for John's complete surrender in the thirteenth century.

The king was the more dependent on his political authority in that he had lost one of the most valuable assets of William I. Though a strong ruler could be sure of the acquiescence of the majority, he could no longer count on the unanimity of ecclesiastical opinion to support him; in fact, the most conscientious were usually opposed to him. This change had begun with the small band of adherents that joined Anselm. Stephen's reign provided the opportunity for this party to expand, and it contained the leaders of the Church in its ranks; finally, though still a minority, it was a very formidable minority under Becket. I have no doubt that monasticism played its part in this, though I am not prepared to give it so large a part as Heinrich Böhmer has portrayed. But the ambition of great monasteries to be exempt from episcopal control naturally made them supporters of papal authority. This authority was certainly championed by the newer Orders, among which the Cistercians especially spread over England with great rapidity; here, as elsewhere, St Bernard's dominating influence was felt. But there is another factor which to my mind is the most important of all—the law of the Church. I have already shown that from the time of the Conquest all the collections of ecclesiastical law, complete or abridged, included and made prominent the extreme claims to papal authority that were being put forward at Rome. Only a limited number of the clergy did study these and make themselves familiar with the laws of the Church, but those who did could not fail to notice and to be impressed by the canons that enforced obedience to Rome. Lanfranc had introduced the first of these collections into England; it had been widely disseminated and he had encouraged its study. Soon there were further collections, each adding something to the last, a continued progress along the same road. After Lanfranc, archbishop Theobald (1139–61) gave the next great impulse to the study of ecclesiastical law, which becomes much more general in consequence. When we come to the great Becket controversy, we cannot but be struck by the fact that even the ecclesiastical opponents of Becket recognise the papal authority to the full. This it was that put them at a disadvantage and ensured their defeat.

In the reign of Henry I there was little external sign of change. He had had to yield on the question of lay investiture, but had otherwise maintained his control over episcopal (and abbatial) elections, and he had skilfully twisted Paschal II's temporary concession that consecration might follow homage into a permanent rule that homage must precede consecration. The details of episcopal elections under Henry I show that he acted exactly as Henry II in the Constitutions of Clarendon said that he did. He was equally determined to maintain his authority in other respects too, especially to keep intact the barrier that his father had interposed between England and Rome. No papal legates or letters were to be admitted without his sanction; appeals to Rome were similarly prohibited; and ecclesiastical synods were under his direct supervision.[1] Actually, however, he was not in so strong a position as his father. First of all, there had been opposition to his policy in England. And,

[1] Cf. my article in the Cambridge Historical Journal, vol. II, p. 214.

secondly, in the matter of Church reform he was suspect. After Anselm's death he allowed the see of Canterbury to remain vacant for five years, and reaped financial advantages therefrom; while his zeal against the married clergy seemed to be prompted not by religious feeling but by the desire to extract fines from the offenders. Therefore the Papacy was the more anxious to put the work of reform in the hands of its own legates.

The history of papal legates in England is most instructive; it shows that the king had constantly to be on the alert, and that the situation was far more difficult for Henry I than it had been for William I. Trouble began with the election of Ralph, bishop of Rochester, to the archbishopric of Canterbury in 1114, which necessitated recourse to Rome for the pallium. The Pope for some time refused to recognise the election; he was especially indignant that his sanction had not been obtained, as canon law required, for the translation of Ralph to his new see. The intercession of Anselm, abbot of Santa Saba at Rome and nephew of the great Anselm, was effective in inducing Paschal II to yield; Anselm, already well known in England, was himself sent with the pallium. But he was also sent with papal letters denouncing the barrier interposed by the king between England and Rome, and this put Henry on his guard. When Anselm was sent again as papal legate in 1116, he was refused admission into England, and remained for three years in Normandy, an honoured but a helpless guest. In 1119 Henry had an interview with the new Pope, Calixtus II, at Gisors, where he put forward the claim that, by a custom of the country, no legatine authority could be exercised in England, unless the king himself desired it in order to settle some particular dispute or to deal with some matter which the archbishop and bishops could not settle on their own authority. Eadmer[1] asserts that Calixtus II conceded this claim. It sounds almost incredible; at any rate Calixtus did not refrain from sending legates. One, Peter Pierleone, was admitted by Henry in 1121, but only that the king might repeat his claim to him; he performed no legatine act.[2] It therefore is most surprising to find that in 1125 John of Crema was allowed to enter, and that he actually held a legatine Council at Westminster. The canons of this Council introduced no novelty[3]—they were mainly directed to the reform of the lower clergy, especially the enforcement of clerical celibacy—but the holding of a Council by a papal legate was a great innovation.[4] Such a thing had not happened since the beginning of William I's reign, and then only because, for the changes that William desired in the English Church, papal legates were necessary; they were not necessary now, and it shocked conservative opinion, as the chroniclers describe, to see the two archbishops taking a subordinate position to one who was only in priest's orders. For some reason Henry had found it impossible to main-

[1] *Historia Novorum*, p. 258.

[2] *Ib.* pp. 295–6.

[3] Except that they repeated some of the canons of the First Lateran Council.

[4] Gilbert Foliot (*Epp.*, ed. Giles, J.A., vol. I, pp. 282–283) recognises that John of Crema acted contrary to the "customs" of the country. He compares his methods, however, very favourably with those of Becket.

tain his principle of isolation,[1] and thereby he yielded something more vital than lay investiture.

Probably the holding of a council by the legate, the thing he would be most anxious to prevent, came as a surprise to him (he was not himself in England), and made him the more urgent in pressing upon the Pope the granting of legatine authority to the archbishop of Canterbury, which had long been sought by king and archbishops. This was at last conceded by Honorius II in 1126, and it was a compromise that gave satisfaction to both sides. The Pope obtained a standing legate in England, to whom he could send his instructions, and so ensure that reform was under his direction. Lanfranc and Anselm had presided over councils of all the bishops of the kingdom. Archbishops of Canterbury in future could only preside over a council of the bishops of their province, unless they were papal legates. The Council held by William in 1127, which promulgated reforming canons, was a legatine Council. Also the appointment was only given to an individual, it did not go with the office; and it became void on the death of the Pope who conferred it. It was only a temporary concession, which did not bind future Popes. However, it was of considerable value to the king, because it did away with the recurrent danger of the appearance of legates from Rome, and he could ensure that the archbishop

---

[1] Tillman, H., *Die päpstlichen Legaten in England bis zur Beendigung der Legation Gualas* (1218), p. 28, suggests that Henry allowed this legation because he felt under an obligation to the legate, who had dissolved the marriage of Henry's nephew William Clito with the daughter of Fulk of Anjou, on the grounds of consanguinity. This marriage would have united two of Henry's most dangerous enemies.

did not promulgate canons without his approval.
We are told that he expressly gave his consent to the
canons of 1127. It also gave an ecclesiastical unity to
the Church in England, and it soothed the feelings of
the archbishop, deeply wounded by his failure to
obtain the primacy over York. It therefore was a
temporary solution, not only of the question of papal
legates, but also of the vexed question between
Canterbury and York.

That long struggle, which had just been decided in
favour of York, concerns us here only indirectly.
Henry I, it is true, had strongly supported archbishop
Ralph, and had for a long time refused to admit into
England archbishop Thurstan of York, formerly one
of his chaplains, because Thurstan had obtained
consecration from the Pope and so had successfully
evaded the profession of obedience demanded by the
archbishop of Canterbury. The king was naturally on
the side of unification. One head of the Church in
England was much more satisfactory to him than
two; it made for better government and the easier
working of his own authority. But, though he tried to
influence the decision of the papal court, he never
denied its competency to settle the question. This is a
good example of the recognition by the king of the
papal headship of the Church. It was a question that
could not be decided by the English ecclesiastical
courts; it had, therefore, to be referred to the papal
court. And it remained throughout strictly a legal
question, which turned on precedents and previous
judgments of Popes, and was decided accordingly. It
has been argued that the Popes were opposed to the

uniting of the Church of England under one head for
the very reasons that caused the king of England to
favour it, and that this motive induced them to decide
for York. On the other hand, the creation of primacies had been a definite feature of the centralising
policy of the Papacy from the time of Gregory VII;
and even in a kingdom, for Urban II had granted the
primacy in Spain to the archbishop of Toledo, as the
restoration of an old right.

Spain was no longer a single kingdom, but the old
right is restored in its old sphere. The question in
England was whether the primacy was an old right
attaching to the see of Canterbury. It had been
referred to Rome by William I, and Pope Alexander
II had referred it back to England to be decided on the
question of fact. Lanfranc had convinced William
and the Council by his eloquence and his evidence,
and Alexander seems to have accepted the decision
and to have been satisfied with the account given by
Lanfranc.[1] But no actual confirmation came from
Rome, and the archbishops of York were not satisfied.
The dispute arose again, and added another to the
burdens of Anselm. It was unlike him to feel so
strongly upon a matter of this kind; probably he was
roused to action by the zeal of the Canterbury monks,
who were determined to counter the rival zeal of the

[1] Lanfranc told the Pope what the evidence was, but, as he
refrains from specifying it among his other enclosures, he probably
did not send it. There is no reason why he should have done so,
because the Pope had left the question of fact to be decided in
England. The judgment on questions of fact was commonly delegated
to the country of origin. If the evidence was not sent, we have an
explanation of (1) why the forgery was not exposed at once, (2) why
the Pope did not issue an official confirmation of the English verdict.

York chapter urging on their archbishop. During Anselm's lifetime the situation was abnormal; the king was hostile, but the Pope upheld him in return for his devoted loyalty to the Papacy. But, after his death, the king returned to the side of Canterbury and the Pope began to listen to the arguments of the York party. They had valuable evidence in letters of Gregory I and Honorius I, and all the eloquence of archbishop Ralph was unable to explain these away. Moreover, the onus of proof rested with Canterbury, and when the papal letters produced in evidence by the archbishop were exposed as forgeries, the verdict was bound to be against him. Archbishop William of Canterbury received a solatium in the grant of the papal legation, so that as legate he regained what he had lost as archbishop.

There is no reason to believe that the Popes acted on other than judicial grounds in the settlement of this question. But the circumstances gave them opportunities which they made use of to advance their own authority, where heretofore it had been exceptionally weak—over the English episcopate. The length of the dispute, and the persistence of the king to obtain the decision he wanted, resulted in frequent reference to Rome. The archbishops, and both their representatives and the king's, were constantly visiting the Pope. It was therefore no longer unusual for English bishops to appear at Rome, and they were even present (and English abbots also) at Councils, at Rheims and elsewhere, presided over by the Pope.[1] This had not happened, except in rare cases, such as Anselm, since

[1] Cf. Böhmer, H., *Kirche und Staat*, p. 299, n. 4.

the Conquest, and from the point of view of the king
it was especially to be avoided; the contact of English
bishops with the Pope was even more dangerous than
the presence of a legate in England.

Too much, however, must not be made of what
were exceptions to the general rule. As I said before,
there was little external sign of change during Henry's
reign. His position was such that he could command
obedience from all his subjects. But when a papal
legate could preside over a council in England, and
English bishops attend councils presided over by the
Pope, there were obvious gaps in the barrier which
had been interposed especially to prevent these contacts. Discontent with Henry's ecclesiastical policy
was not vocal after the death of Anselm, but it was
certainly alive and was indicated immediately after his
death. Doubtless he still had the majority of the
ecclesiastical officials, his own nominees, behind him,
and he also had the powerful support of custom. But
in the last resort his authority over the Church depended on political strength, and in the political weakness of the succeeding reign the king lost that authority. The death of Henry I, therefore, marks the end
of a period in Church history. The situation in England
under the Norman kings was never again to be exactly
repeated.

CHAPTER XII

STEPHEN. THE "FREEDOM OF THE CHURCH"

THE strong hand of the Norman kings had kept the English Church in the old groove, in which they considered it should remain, as an integral part of the Church as a whole; but the Church as they conceived it was the Church as it had been at the beginning of the eleventh century, not as it actually was. Many ecclesiastics acquiesced in the royal conception, but quite a number, and those among the best, felt the control of Henry I to be a tyranny and longed to be free from it. This, though it had not been evident before, became so immediately after his death. A weak ruler and a disputed succession gave them their opportunity, and the claim is emphatically pressed for the freedom of the English Church. What, then, was this claim? What is implied by the "freedom of the Church"? To modern minds it means freedom from State control, and, as a consequence of that, the freedom of self-government possessed by an independent, and in this case, national Church. This is the way that many people view the claim put forward in the twelfth century; this it is that makes Becket appear to them as a national hero. But the claim was not really for freedom in that sense, though certainly freedom from lay control was in the very essence of the claim. It had begun, more humbly, as an appeal for freedom from particular abuses, the special innovations of a deleterious nature that had been intro-

duced. Thus Henry I, promising in his charter a
restoration of the good old customs, began with the
promise of freedom to the Church, and explained
what he meant by saying that he would not lay hands
on Church property, even during the vacancy of a see.
The Church was to have the freedom it had enjoyed
under William I. He did not keep his promise, and he
travelled far from the reforming policy of his father;
unwisely, for the general desire for reform was more
ardent, and the influence of Rome more effective.

Stephen, who was deeply beholden to the Church
and to the Papacy for his elevation to the throne, also
promised freedom to the Church in his charter of
1136, but freedom is now given a much more broad
interpretation. Simony was not to enter into any of
his dealings with the Church; the control of ecclesiastical jurisdiction and ecclesiastical property was to be
in the hands of the bishops; all possessions of churches
were to be restored as they were at the time of
William I's death; the old practices of *regalia* and
spolia were to be abolished. Finally, Stephen indirectly recognised freedom of canonical election.
Henry I had promised in 1100 that he would not
exercise the right of regalia during a vacancy, *donec
successor in eam ingrediatur*; Stephen promised the
same, *donec pastor canonice substituatur*. There was
some ground for Henry of Huntingdon's statement,
which has often been challenged, that he promised not
to interfere with elections. At any rate, non-inter-
ference with the Church was what was expected from
Stephen. Freedom had now come to mean both
freedom from lay control and freedom to obey the

CH. XII]STEPHEN177

laws of the Church, especially the new reforming decrees, freedom, in fact, to be as the rest of the Church was. The hand of the secular tyrant was to be removed. What was to take its place? The English Church was not, and did not wish to be, independent. If it was to be as the rest of the Church, it must obey the law of the Church; and, since that law, in England as elsewhere, emphasised throughout the primacy of the Church of Rome, the sovereign authority of the Pope in all things and over all persons ecclesiastical, it must logically accept that sovereignty and be obedient to its dictates. This was recognised, at any rate by the leading personalities. Theobald, who was archbishop of Canterbury during all but the first four years of the reign, had no doubts about it. Henry of Blois, bishop of Winchester and papal legate, who had been bishop for six years before Stephen's accession and who survived to outlive Becket, accepted it without question. And Stephen himself can have had no illusions about it. He was indebted to the Pope more heavily than to anyone, and the immediate assertion of papal authority in England was not challenged by him. The Pope, of course, took it for granted, and acted accordingly.

Now the Popes had always expected something more from England than the normal obedience which they claimed from the Church as a whole. First of all, the English Church owed its foundation and its organisation to the Roman Church, for it was Pope Gregory the Great who had sent Augustine and had directed him in the government of the new Church. This early subordination was never forgotten or

BEC12

denied, and references to it are constantly cropping up throughout our period. If Rome was the mother of all the churches, she was in a particular sense the mother of the English Church. Secondly, England recognised a pecuniary obligation to Rome of an unusual kind, the annual payment of a silver penny from each hearth, the Peter's Pence,[1] which amounted to a total of 300 marks save one—£199. 6s. 8d.—each year. This the Papacy called a *census* and treated it as such, that is to say, a feudal payment in return for protection, and therefore implying a feudal overlordship which demanded fealty in return. William I had owned to the one and disowned the other, but the Papacy continued to link them together. Urban II wrote[2] in this sense to Lanfranc in 1088, but as William II had refused to recognise Urban there was no occasion to answer him. Paschal II raised the claim again in 1101, when he instructed Anselm to give his mind more effectively to the *fidelitas* due from the king and to the restoration of the *census* of St Peter.[3] The bishops were responsible for their diocesan contributions, and, these being fixed in amount, they, like all tax-gatherers of the time, usually collected a surplus for their own pockets, as Innocent III complained most bitterly. But the payments, which were never made regularly, depended on the king, and the Pope had to negotiate with him. The kings did frequently enforce or authorise the payment, but they

---

[1] Cf., on this subject, Jensen, O., *The "Denarius Sancti Petri" in England* (Transactions of the Royal Historical Society, New Series, vols. XV and XIX).

[2] Jaffé-Löwenfeld, 5351.

[3] Anselm, *Epistolae*, III, 42; Jaffé-Löwenfeld, 5883.

never accepted the papal inference; it remained, however, always in the minds of the Popes.

So, then, the Popes expected the obedience of a daughter from the English Church, and from the kingdom a recognition of its subordination. The disputed election on Henry I's death, and its reference to the papal court, was for the Papacy a satisfactory beginning of a new regime. Stephen, though recognition of him was fairly general in England, was anxious for this sanction, and it was necessary for his supporters, because the Pope alone could grant a general absolution from the oath they had all taken to Matilda in Henry's lifetime. John of Salisbury in his *Historia Pontificalis* (c. 42) gives a graphic description of the enquiry at the papal court, and hints very broadly that Stephen's money won him the final verdict. It would probably be truer to say that the papal judgment was influenced rather by ecclesiastical than by judicial considerations; the arguments put forward by Stephen's representatives were certainly not convincing, and the Pope seems to have made up his mind beforehand.[1] This reference to Rome created an important precedent, and later the Pope was able to take the initiative without waiting for the case to be referred to him. When Stephen had fallen into ill-favour with the Church, the Pope prohibited the coronation of his son Eustace; the success of his prohibition ensured the

---

[1] This is explained by Dr R. L. Poole in his edition of the *Historia Pontificalis* (Appendix VI), who shows that Stephen's election had been confirmed at once by the Pope, and that the enquiry at Rome was held in consequence of Matilda's appeal. The hearing took place at the Second Lateran Council in 1139. Both in this passage and elsewhere, John of Salisbury's bias against Stephen must be taken into account, and his rather impish delight in retailing malicious gossip.

throne to Henry II, the son of that Matilda against
whom the verdict had previously been given.

There had been an earlier precedent, when William
I had obtained papal sanction for his conquest of
England, but on that occasion the appeal had come
from one side only and the other side had not been
represented at the papal court. William, however, had
been careful to ensure that the Papacy should claim
nothing in return. Papal legates appeared in England
almost at once to reform and reorganise the Church,
but they were there by royal invitation because their
presence was essential to William's purpose. Stephen,
having already received papal confirmation, as he was
careful to state, issued his promise of freedom to the
English Church, and the Papacy was able to act on its
own authority and without invitation. Once more the
tale of papal legates is instructive and symptomatic.
There was a standing legate already in the person of
William, archbishop of Canterbury, whose legation
had been continued by Innocent II, but after his
death in 1136 a cardinal, Alberic, was sent as legate
from Rome. He made a regular visitation of most of
the bishoprics and abbeys in England, and held an
important legatine Council in 1138; its canons deal
again with reform, but more stringently than before,
and two of the canons (nos. 7 and 10) are noteworthy
for the reference to the Pope on which they insist; thus,
if anyone lays violent hands on clerk or monk, he is
not, unless on the point of death, to receive absolution
save from the Pope alone.[1] And, finally, Alberic gave

[1] This was also passed the following year at the Second Lateran
Council (canon 15), to which Alberic went on his return from England.

his sanction to the election of Theobald, and himself consecrated him archbishop of Canterbury.

Stephen, who acquiesced in all this, was probably as anxious as his predecessor to prevent it, but he lacked the power. It was, therefore, a matter of considerable satisfaction to him that, after the departure of Alberic, the Pope consented again to the appointment of a standing legate, and also acceded to Stephen's desire in appointing, not the new archbishop of Canterbury, but Stephen's own brother, Henry of Blois, the bishop of Winchester. The king's satisfaction, however, was short-lived. He would have done better to press the claim of the archbishop of Canterbury in accordance with precedent; it did not make for harmony in the Church when the archbishop had to take a subordinate position to one of the bishops of his own province. He would even have done better without a standing legate, for a legate sent *a latere* would not have been permanent, and would certainly not have had the political influence which Henry of Blois was able to exercise.

Henry was an ambitious man, not in the least disposed to act in accordance with the royal will. On the contrary, he took the lead in putting Matilda on the throne, and again in restoring Stephen. To the Pope he was obedient, as it was from the Pope that his authority was derived, and he used this authority to the full. During the four years of his legation he acted as master of the English Church. He held a legatine council in 1143[1] and legatine visitations, and

[1] Böhmer, *Kirche und Staat*, p. 346, n. 5, is probably right in assigning to this council the canons printed in Wilkins, *Concilia*, vol. 1,

promoted Church reform with great zeal. Further, he supervised and controlled appointments to bishoprics and abbeys, and even acted in the stead of the archbishop of Canterbury by performing himself the metropolitan functions of examination and consecration. Though he faithfully served papal interests,[1] his ambition may have been viewed with suspicion at Rome; St Bernard was certainly not favourably disposed towards him. At any rate, with Innocent II's death in 1143 his legation came to an end; though he went himself to Rome to plead his cause, Innocent's successors refused to renew the appointment. Lucius II sent a cardinal-bishop, Imar, as legate to England with full powers, but the normal situation was restored when Eugenius III, about the year 1150, appointed the archbishop of Canterbury, Theobald, as standing legate; the appointment was renewed by succeeding Popes, so that Theobald remained as legate until his death in 1161. This still did not improve the position from the king's point of view, as Theobald, who held a legatine council in 1151, acted throughout as papal agent and took his orders from the Pope. He did not display any signs of personal ambition, but, endowed with the legatine as well as

p. 417. Of them three insist on reference to Rome, though this fact is obscured in Wilkins' text, as he has twice misread "domino papa" of the MS. as "domino proprio".

[1] Among other things he saw to the collection of Peter's Pence. There is a letter (in British Museum MS. Cotton. Vespasian E, iv, f. 203ᵛ), addressed by him as legate to the prior and monastery of Worcester in the absence of the bishop, blaming them for the non-receipt of their quota, and saying that all the other dioceses had sent theirs. He threatens an interdict if the money is not paid within fifteen days.

the metropolitan dignity, he, and not the king, was clearly the master of the Church in England. By no change of legates was Stephen in the least benefited.

The appointments to bishoprics and abbeys had passed out of the king's hands. Theobald was Stephen's choice for the archbishopric of Canterbury in 1139, and Matilda had established Robert de Sigillo as bishop of London in 1141. Otherwise the royal authority was singularly ineffective. Henry of Winchester had practically controlled appointments during the four years of his legation. After 1143, when he ceased to be legate, the noticeable feature at elections is freedom in the canonical sense,[1] so that the chapters really chose their bishops; and, further, the supervision was in the hands of the archbishop of Canterbury, who both ensured canonical election and carried out his own canonical duties of examination and consecration. But canonical election was not without its difficulties. Quarrels among the electors and disputed elections were not infrequent,[2] so that a not uncommon result was appeal to Rome. In a number of cases it was papal authority that finally decided the election, and sometimes, for instance at the election of Richard of Belmeis to London in 1152, about which Gilbert Foliot wrote (ep. 94) in rather fulsome terms to the Pope, the Papacy intervened decisively to prevent baronial interference, which was more dangerous now than royal. The king's confirmation of the election was only a formality, and there is not sufficient

---

[1] Cf. Böhmer, H., *Kirche und Staat*, pp. 371 foll.; Tillmann, H., *Die päpstliche Legaten*, p. 46, n. 180.

[2] Böhmer, *op. cit.* p. 390.

evidence to show whether the bishop-elect did homage
to the king; the presumption, mainly from silence, is
that this had ceased and that the king had to be content
with the oath of fealty.[1] On one point in the accustomed procedure Stephen was more inclined to assert
himself: he insisted on the necessity of the royal
licence to elect. But this was very different from the
practice of his predecessors, whose licence had usually
been as definite as a *congé d'élire* to-day. Stephen,
however, seems to have reaped financial advantages
out of it, as he charged 500 marks for the licence, if
we are to believe John of Salisbury,[2] who quotes as
instances the elections of Richard of Belmeis to the
bishopric of London and Silvester to the abbey of
St Augustine, Canterbury. This, if true, exposed
Stephen to the charge of simony, a breach of his
charter and an offence against the freedom of the
Church.

In another direction, besides its influence over
elections, papal authority was obtaining a firm footing
in this country. The monasteries were always inclined
to the Papacy: they were anxious to secure papal
protection and confirmation of their possessions,
paying a small *census* in return; and some of them
even obtained exemption from episcopal control. This
was always the case with the Cluniac foundations, and
soon came to be with the Cistercian as well. The older
Benedictine monasteries were anxious for the same
privilege, which in their case meant much greater
autonomy, each monastery being an independent

[1] Böhmer, *op. cit.* p. 390, n. 5.
[2] *Historia Pontificalis*, pp. 89–91.

unit. St Augustine's, Canterbury, was at constant strife with the archbishop about its privileges, and Lanfranc had dealt with it very harshly in consequence; it was still at feud with the archbishop in Theobald's day. Evesham was another of the older monasteries that was jealous of its rights; it had a set of forged privileges from earlier Popes to support them. These are only instances to illustrate the general tendency; it would be very interesting if we had a complete list of those older monasteries which possessed papal privileges. However, not many monasteries dared to assert their independence in Lanfranc's day, in face of his forcible assertion of episcopal rights; but besides St Augustine's we hear of Bury rousing his ire by obtaining exemption from Alexander II, and of his refusal to allow the privilege to be exercised.[1] In Henry I's reign we get some more instances. Bury again vindicates its exemption from the bishop of Thetford, in spite of his personal visit to the Pope.[2] We also hear of the great abbey of Gloucester receiving protection and confirmation of its privileges from Honorius II,[3] and a secular chapter takes the same step when the church of Hereford obtains a similar privilege from Innocent II.[4] One or two other instances could be adduced, but the total number does not appear to be large.

What was the exception in Henry I's reign, however, begins to be the rule under Stephen. I have elsewhere given some instances of this,[5] and Miss Rose

[1] See above, p. 131, n. 1.
[2] Eadmer, *Historia Novorum*, pp. 132–133.
[3] Jaffé-Löwenfeld, 7340.   [4] *Ib.* 7525.
[5] Cambridge Historical Journal, vol. II, p. 215.

Graham has supplied a fuller list.[1] It was a natural result of the civil war that the ecclesiastical corporations should look to the Head of the Church for the protection which the secular ruler was no longer able to ensure. But it is the more important in that monasticism was becoming increasingly influential in the English Church. The number of monasteries was rapidly increasing: the Norman kings had set the fashion, which the nobles had followed, of founding and endowing monasteries; then came the introduction of the new Orders and the especially rapid spread of the Cistercian Order. This increase in numbers was accompanied by an increase of influence also, owing to the quickening of the movement of reform, to which these newcomers especially contributed. Already monasticism had an exceptional position in the English Church, since so many cathedral chapters were monastic. Now parishes as well as cathedrals come under monastic control, and this gave a prospect of better results in the way of reform. For the repeated efforts of archbishops and legates, and the repeated decrees of Councils, had hardly broken the crust of English custom. The reformers had particularly concentrated their efforts to oppose clerical marriage and the control of churches by laymen, but with little result. The parish clergy continued to marry, and, what was more important, to hand on their benefices to their sons, treating their churches as property to be bequeathed like any other possession. Lay patronage helped to make this possible, and there weighed on the Church the heavy hand of lay ownership, with the

[1] *English Ecclesiastical Studies*, p. 185, n. 4.

holding of Church property, even tithes, by laymen. The patron expected his nominee to be instituted as a matter of course, and the bishops had a hard fight to get any recognition of their right to investigate the fitness of a candidate. The substitution of monastic for lay patrons was therefore a considerable step in advance, and the bishops as a whole seem to have encouraged such transfers. At any rate, as Professor Stenton says:[1] "in the twelfth century hundreds of parish churches throughout England passed into the possession of the religious". Whether this worked ultimately for the well-being of the Church is extremely doubtful, but the immediate advantage was considerable; and it cannot be denied that it had the effect of making the monasteries still more important in the life of the Church, increasing both their influence and their revenues. And the extension of their influence meant an extension also of papal authority.

Now, while on the one hand the king had to acquiesce in the gradual loss of his control over the Church, on the other hand he had often to submit, even in political matters, to the dictation of the Church. The bishops, who were now papal rather than royal officials, could yet intervene decisively in political affairs; as in ninth-century France the weakness of the royal power gave them their opportunity. Stephen could not even take action against bishops who were politically dangerous to him. His attack on the arrogant bishop of Salisbury, Roger, and his nephew Alexander of Lincoln led to the cry that the freedom of the Church was in danger. The episcopate closed

---

[1] Cambridge Historical Journal, vol. III, p. 1.

its ranks, and with Stephen's brother at its head brought about the defeat of the king. He recovered power with their help again, for Matilda was much more formidable and dangerous to freedom, but he never recovered the full favour of the Church. When the political situation improved, he tried to assert some authority in ecclesiastical matters, and there were murmurs that he was infringing his charter by laying hands on Church property and attempting to interfere in elections. In 1148 he took a more decisive step. He would only allow three bishops to attend the Council at Rheims presided over by Pope Eugenius III, and he definitely forbade the attendance of archbishop Theobald. Theobald went, notwithstanding the prohibition, and when Stephen confiscated the archbishop's temporalities and banished him to France, the Pope pronounced an interdict. Stephen on this occasion seems to have had some of the bishops on his side, but he had to yield and make his peace with the archbishop. By his belated attempt to regain the initiative he had forfeited ecclesiastical support; the Pope forbade the coronation of his son Eustace, and Theobald left the country rather than perform the ceremony. When Eustace suddenly died, Stephen resigned himself to the inevitable and recognised Henry II as his heir. Once again the Church had imposed its will.

So the "freedom of the Church" was achieved. Stephen had failed entirely to maintain the barrier set up by his predecessors. Papal bulls and papal legates freely entered the country; ecclesiastical synods and episcopal and abbatial elections were out of the

king's control. In spite of his prohibition bishops
obeyed the papal summons, and ecclesiastical suits
were taken to Rome without his leave being sought.
The right of any ecclesiastic to appeal to the Pope was
one of the cardinal doctrines in every collection of
Church law. The practice began in England in the
reign of Stephen, and the early letters of Gilbert
Foliot show it in operation. It was at present only a
beginning; the majority of cases would still probably
be settled in the English courts;[1] but it was so far
established that it continued unimpeded during the
first years of Henry II's reign, in fact until the death
of archbishop Theobald.

Nor was this the only novelty that continued up to
that date. It is a signal testimony to the importance of
Theobald that in the history of the English Church
the date that matters is not the death of the king,
Stephen, but the death of the archbishop of Canterbury, Theobald. Henry II was deeply indebted to the
Church for the ease and security of his succession; yet
it was rather policy than gratitude that caused him to
bide his time until Theobald was dead. The archbishop appears to have been a quiet self-effacing man,
without personal ambition, and a willing servant of
the Pope, whom he obeyed unquestioningly. But, like
Anselm, he was not for that reason insignificant. Far
from it. He was, moreover, renowned for his learning,
especially in the law of the Church. He has been
described as the founder of canonical jurisprudence in

[1] I argued this in the Cambridge Historical Journal, vol. II, p. 223,
and my view was supported by Professor F. M. Stenton, in the same
journal, vol. III, p. 3, who arrived at the same conclusion from
different evidence.

England. I have shown that Lanfranc laid the foundations for the knowledge of the law, but Theobald was the first of his successors to build upon these foundations. Lanfranc had adjured the bishops to study the canons and the decrees of the Popes, and had provided them with the material. Theobald, by adding to the material and improving the method, did more even than Lanfranc to ensure the proper knowledge and study of Church law. He had a circle of students round him, and from his household came some of the leading ecclesiastics of the next reign. He was the third archbishop of Canterbury to come from Bec, and as his two great predecessors he left his mark on the English Church. He was like Anselm in character and in obedience to the Pope, like Lanfranc in his legal bent; and the study of ecclesiastical law was an essential in the new order of things in the Church. So far as I can discover, the collection introduced by Lanfranc into England was the only complete collection that existed in this country for half a century, perhaps even three-quarters; I have shown that it was widely diffused. It begins now to be superseded by fuller, more up-to-date collections, arranged in a systematic form. For some of this Theobald must have been responsible, perhaps for the major part. At any rate, the existence of these collections in England is certain; and it is evident that a new impulse had been given to the study of ecclesiastical law. The effect of this is markedly felt in the great controversy which raged during the years immediately following the death of Theobald; Becket owed to Theobald not only his early training but also his eventual success.

CHAPTER XIII

HENRY II AND THOMAS BECKET

T HE preservation of the barrier against papal interference with the English Church had, in the time of the first three Norman kings, depended partly on their political strength, partly on the support they received from the episcopate. Henry II had a far more formidable task than they, for he had to exclude the papal authority which had obtained so firm a footing in Stephen's reign, and to rebuild again the barrier which had been broken down. Physical force alone was insufficient; he was much more dependent than his predecessors on the goodwill of the English bishops. Therefore the conflict with Becket came at a most awkward moment for him. Ultimately it ruined his scheme; it was the determining factor which prevented the barrier from being rebuilt. Henry was handicapped, because, though he could reckon on the goodwill of the ecclesiastical officials as a whole, he could not reckon on their undivided allegiance. The doctrines of the Canon Law were known and could not be gainsaid; and for over twenty years a new practice had superseded the old tradition of obedience to the sovereign. As a prelude to the story of the great conflict, a prelude essential to the right understanding of what took place, I want to attempt an estimate of the principal actors in the drama, Becket himself and his supporters, and also his opponents as well; and to consider them principally in relation to my main theme, to see how they stood between the rival claims on their allegiance of Pope and king.

I feel it is a rash venture to attempt an estimate of Becket, about whom so much has been written from his own time to the present. So many portraits have been drawn of him: he has been viewed through many different spectacles, tinged with national colours or ecclesiastical of varied hues, and in the glory cast by the halo of exile and martyrdom. His career presents the most striking contrasts: first, the rising young ecclesiastic in Theobald's household, undoubtedly a favourite with the archbishop; then, the worldly chancellor, the jovial companion of the king, pluralist and despoiler of Church property; finally, the archbishop who will fiercely prevent any infringement of his rights and privileges, his courts and his possessions, and at the same time the exalted champion of the "freedom of the Church" and of papal authority, as stern and as dictatorial as St Bernard himself had been. No wonder that his contemporaries formed wrong impressions of him. His former master, Theobald, who loved him, was in his last days full of distress at the worldliness into which he had lapsed, and tried in vain to recall him to his duties as archdeacon. The greatest and most fatal misjudgment was the king's, but who could expect such a chancellor to change into such an archbishop? This was indeed the difficulty which his admirers, and especially his biographers, had to get over. Neither the miracle of a sudden conversion, nor the theory that he had been dissimulating as chancellor in order to use his influence for good with the king, are explanations that seem at all satisfactory in his case. On the other hand, his opponents, such as Gilbert Foliot, regarded him as a hypocrite, insincere and swollen with pride. Their accusations are as unsatisfactory as the excuses of his friends.

The only explanation of him that seems to me to fit the facts at all is that he was one of those men who, exalting to the full the rôle they have to play, picture themselves as the perfect representatives of their office, visualising a type and making themselves the living impersonation of it; actors playing a part, but unconscious actors. He was of a romantic turn of mind, with a vivid imagination and enough knowledge of the past to give his imagination scope. As chancellor, he was the perfect king's servant, a splendid companion as well as a splendid servant, subordinating everything to the king's will, indispensable to his master; and withal leading a perfectly moral life. When he was appointed archbishop, it needed no miraculous conversion; he pictured himself in the part at once, and he warned the king of the consequences. He threw off the layman and became the complete archbishop. At first this was the extent of his rôle, but as events changed he developed. He pictured himself as one of the Church's heroes, patiently resisting the tyrant on behalf of the freedom of the Church, submitting to adversity and exile, enduring, nay welcoming, martyrdom at the last; and though the natural man in him kept breaking out in violent outbursts and fierce denunciations of his opponents, this was also to some extent in keeping with his part. I do not for a moment suggest that he was insincere, or that he was merely playing a part. He was living a part, and it was absolutely real to him, so much so that his partisans saw him as he saw himself; no mere actor could have become the great martyr-saint of the English Church. But I think he was often, in consequence, blind to the practical facts of the situation, and to the entirely unnecessary irritation that he so often aroused.

Most people have pictured themselves in positions of importance, and how easy it is in such dreams to attain the perfection of composure, dignified authority, and command of the situation. Becket was one of the rare persons who could translate his dreams into realities. People have often commented on the great change in him when he turned from chancellor into archbishop; but this was really less violent a change than the previous one from Theobald's clerk into chancellor. It was not after all so strange that he should easily become the great archbishop. He had lived in an archbishop's circle, and moved in higher circles still when he went with Theobald to the papal Council at Rheims; then he had seen Theobald defy King Stephen and vindicate the archiepiscopal rights. At Rheims he may have pictured himself as Pope. He had certainly pictured himself as archbishop; he knew what he would be like, and he warned Henry of the consequences if he became archbishop. His dreams had been exalted dreams. He magnified to the full the office in which he saw himself. And, unfortunately, he became obsessed with its importance, its rights and its privileges. His conception was essentially grandiose. One wonders what would have been the

character of his tenure of the archbishopric if it had
been a peaceful one.

The man who came nearest to understanding him
was John of Salisbury, the sanest and most clear-
headed of his contemporaries, though he is sometimes
labelled cautious and academic. He obviously felt
sincere affection for Becket, and he realised his ability
and value as chancellor, even though he disapproved
of some of his actions. John had been a papal clerk and
a secretary of archbishop Theobald, and was naturally a convinced opponent of secular control over the
Church. Yet he deprecated the intransigence of
Becket as archbishop, gently indeed and affectionately,
but as decidedly as he had deprecated his excessive
secularity as chancellor. He tried to persuade him to
come to terms with the king, to compromise and maintain the peace, as the most hopeful way in the long
run. And later on we find him intervening to modify
the violence of letters drafted by the archbishop.
Most characteristic, and surely not typically academic,
was the well-known advice he gave to Becket in May
1165.[1] Becket, in exile at Pontigny, was devoting
himself to the study of canon law, making himself
more perfect in his part, and incidentally collecting
the legal authorities with which to confound his
opponents. John deprecates this study. Law and the
canons are excellent things in their place, but this is
not the time for them. Pondering upon them makes
the mind puffed up; what is needed at this crisis is
a humble heart before God, and this should be

---

[1] *Materials for the history of Archbishop Thomas Becket*, ed.
Robertson, J. C., Rolls Series, vol. v, pp. 161 foll.

cultivated by prayer and spiritual exercise. Better to
discuss right conduct with a spiritually minded man
than to brood over litigious questions; he advises him
to read the psalms and the *Moralia* of Gregory the
Great rather than the canons. Wise advice, but it
did not fit in with Becket's rôle, and he went on with
the preparation of his manifestos for the following
year.

But at any rate John was a faithful friend and convinced of the rightness of Becket's cause, though not
always of the means he took to uphold it. Becket had
a number of such adherents, distinguished like John
for their learning. He had the advantage of succeeding
to Theobald, and to the support of those who had been
trained in Theobald's household. Among the bishops
he had two constant supporters in Bartholomew of
Exeter and Roger of Worcester; and perhaps Henry
of Winchester too was on the same side, though fit-
fully and timidly, for he had kept in the background
ever since he had lost the chief place in the Church.

On the other side were the majority of the bishops,
swayed by fear of the king, by self-interest, or quite
honestly by policy; in many cases it is not easy
to determine the motive. The archbishop of York,
Roger, a former associate of Becket in Theobald's
household, was on personal grounds always on bad
terms with him, and he eagerly seized the opportunity
of Becket's loss of the royal favour to gain privileges
for York and even the office of papal legate for himself. He was most obnoxious to the other side, and
John of Salisbury has some anecdotes about him
which are extremely injurious to his moral character;

yet even he did not dare to assert himself against the
Pope. But the chief personality, and much the most
interesting figure, among the opponents of Becket was
Gilbert Foliot, bishop of London. Formerly a monk
and prior at Cluny, then prior of Abbeville, later abbot
of Gloucester and bishop of Hereford before his translation to London, he was noted for the strictness and
uprightness of his life. The Pope gently cautioned
him against too severe asceticism, for fear his health
should suffer; as bishop of Hereford he had the courage to refuse to administer the see of London for the
king, regarding it as contrary to canon law, though at
the time Becket, according to John of Salisbury, was
not scrupling to administer three vacant sees. Above
all he was famous as a scholar and a lawyer. He seems
to have known something of the civil law, from
which there are quotations in his early letters, and he
sent his young archdeacons to study it at Bologna;
in the canon law he certainly had considerable
experience, especially, as he claims, in ecclesiastical
jurisdiction. In his early and in his later letters, that is
to say both before and after the archbishopric of
Becket, we find him immersed in these questions, and
frequently being called upon by the Pope to act as
judge delegate. The Pope employed him also, when
there was no legate, to arrange for the collection of
Peter's Pence. At the same time the king recognised
his merit and valued his counsel. So Henry was
anxious to have him near at hand as bishop of London,
and the Pope readily agreed to his translation and
continually wrote to him as the person most likely to
influence the king for good. But for Becket he might

198 ENGLAND AND THE PAPACY [PT. II

have been the trusted confidant of both king and
Pope, and he would have been a valuable intermediary
between them. As a lawyer he recognised the competence of the papal authority, and at the same time
the force of custom and what was due to the king.
He was not the man to change his character. He could
never have been the complacent courtier, nor on
the other hand the intransigent archbishop. He was
prepared to admit that the king was going beyond his
rights, but he considered, like John of Salisbury, that
for the Church peace was preferable to privilege, and
he was repelled by the attitude of the archbishop. He
was certainly ambitious, being fully aware of his own
capacity, and there was probably some share of
jealousy in his antipathy to Becket; though after
Becket's death he wrote to the king denying that he
wished to be archbishop. He ranks as a supporter of
the king, but only in opposition to Becket, not to the
Pope. He knew the law of the Church and did not
question its validity, so that he could not impugn
papal authority or refuse submission to it. This is the
novelty of the situation, that the episcopate is mostly
on the king's side but cannot act with him directly
against the Pope. The king has to acquiesce in the
situation, but it is a fatal handicap to him.

There is no need to dwell on the mind of the king.
Like his predecessors he wanted undivided control.
He looked back to the regime of his grandfather
Henry I, regarding the intervening reign as a period
of anarchy and refusing to recognise the practice that
had then grown up. His object was to rebuild the

barriers again, and by excluding the papal authority to revive the royal in its old form.

But he had to act with caution. He was indebted for the ease of his accession to the Pope and to arch-bishop Theobald, and he had to be careful not to antagonise them by too sudden a reaction. Relations with Rome remained for a time as they had been, and there was no interference with appeals. But Henry began slowly to exert his influence on elections, to get a personnel amenable to him, and to insist on their doing homage to him before consecration;[1] moreover, he also, with the aid of his chancellor, Thomas Becket, seized opportunities to employ ecclesiastical revenues to his own advantage. The archbishop of Canterbury, however, mattered most, and when Theobald died in 1161 the opportunity for which he had been waiting seemed to have arrived. The hands of the Pope were tied by his contest with Frederick Barbarossa and the anti-Pope; and in his chancellor Henry had the ideal king's servant, exactly the man he wanted at the head of the English Church. He had no difficulty in getting the bishops, reluctant as many of them were, to assent to the election, or the equally reluctant Canterbury monks, though they yielded with a better grace because their rights in the election were recognised. He had more difficulty with Becket him-self, who warned him honestly that the consequences might not be to his liking, but he failed to understand how serious the warning was. He was set on reviving

---

[1] Thus we hear of Bartholomew, bishop-elect of Exeter, having to wait in 1161 for his consecration until he had done homage to the king.

the old "customs", and so restoring the barriers
maintained by his grandfather. With an archbishop of
his own mind, and he knew Becket so well that he felt
sure of this, who would work with him as Lanfranc
had worked with William I, his success was assured
and the Pope would be helpless.

And then the great change took place. The chancellor was transformed into the archbishop. Henry
was still abroad, and the stories that came from
England did not worry him. He knew his man so well,
and could trust in the gratitude of Becket, who owed
everything to him; he had raised him from nothing
to be the first of his subjects. But directly he arrived
in England he awoke to a realisation of the truth, and
the disillusionment must have been most bitter. Nor
did Becket do anything to soften the blow. He refused
to retain the chancellorship, and he pressed to the full
the rights and dignity of his new office. The king could
not intervene to prevent him from reclaiming castles
and churches belonging to his see which had fallen
into lay hands, but he was grievously offended. Nor
could he prevent Becket from rescuing clergy from the
lay courts, and vindicating the undoubted rights of his
own ecclesiastical court; but Henry thoroughly mis-
trusted the ecclesiastical courts, and for the sake of
good order wanted to see criminous clerks suffer at the
hands of the law the same penalties as lay criminals.
Becket was in the right, for the lay courts had clearly
been exceeding their duties; yet the king had considerable justification for his discontent with the behaviour
of the clergy. It was a question which could easily
have been adjusted by common sense and good feeling

on both sides, but there was no good feeling. The taunts and angry outbursts of the king were replied to by the archbishop with the kind of soft answer that inflames wrath. The king grew more and more enraged, and his impatient temper led him into a fatal precipitancy of action. His mind was set on restoring the former royal authority, and he began to press for a pledge from Becket that he would observe the old customs which his predecessors had observed. Such a pledge, to observe something that was both indefinite and almost certainly contrary to canon law, was clearly an innovation to which Becket could not give a direct affirmative. And then the king determined to reveal his full purpose, and to turn the unwritten customs into written constitutions, thus forcing Becket into a position in which he would be breaking the law if he refused obedience to statutes enacted by the king with the consent of his barons.

The publication of the Constitutions of Clarendon in 1164 gave a full revelation of the mind of the king. The restoration of the royal authority is their purpose, and the opportunity is taken to give a ruling on certain points that might be open to dispute; the actual issue with Becket is dealt with in one clause, but it is not the most important, though it was this issue that had led the king to throw down his general challenge. Because this particular issue had led to the promulgation of the Constitutions, it is round it at first that the controversy rages; but it soon becomes merged in the greater question, which lay between king and Pope rather than between king and archbishop. Henry was stating, so he said, the customs of the country; if they were to be binding and to have the force of law, there are two assumptions that must be taken for granted. One is that what took place in Stephen's reign was done in a time of anarchy and could be ignored; to the king this was obvious, though the Church could hardly be expected to acquiesce. Perhaps this difference of outlook explains the later reference on the papal side to "new" customs, though it was not denied that they represented the practice of Henry I's reign; in that respect they were merely "bad" customs. The second assumption was that the Constitutions were a correct statement of the customs of Henry I's reign. If so, the king was again adopting a perfectly reasonable course, which might well seem to him the best means of enforcing compliance. The correctness of his assertion, therefore, needs first to be tested.

Of the sixteen clauses of the Constitutions, six were tolerated by the Pope, and for our purpose, therefore, need not be taken into consideration. The remaining ten fall into two fairly equal groups: four of them turn on the question as to the exact boundaries between the provinces of the lay and the ecclesiastical courts—a question constantly arising in all countries, and entirely independent of the recognition of papal authority. The other six were far more important, for on them hinged the whole question of papal and royal authority. And in each case we know that the king was definitely repeating the practice of his predecessors. The barriers set up by William I and his successors had not been in the form of written constitutions, but we know enough about them from the writings of Eadmer and others, and from the letters of Popes written in protest against them. Clause IV of the Constitutions accordingly lays down that no ecclesiastical officials are to go out of the country without royal licence, and clause VIII that no appeals are to go beyond the archbishop's court, i.e. to Rome, without the king's consent. Clauses VII and X forbade, as William I had done, that any tenants-in-chief or officials of the king should be excommunicated without his permission; and clause V, with somewhat of the same purpose, prevented the Church from establishing a continued hold over those who had once fallen under its ban. Finally, clause XII regulated the elections of bishops and abbots so as to ensure royal control over them and the due performance of homage before consecration; we know that it is an accurate account of the way in which elections were conducted in Henry I's reign after he had come to terms with Anselm. So with regard to these, the most important clauses of the Constitutions, Henry's claim to be merely repeating the customs of his grandfather seems to be a perfectly correct one.

It is more difficult to be precise about the other four. William I when he issued his ordinance concerning the ecclesiastical courts had made no attempt to define the respective frontiers. The two laws, the two jurisdictions, were to be quite distinct. It can hardly be doubted, however, that he would not allow his own courts to suffer, and that it would seem obvious to him that questions relating to property should be regularly decided in the king's courts. This was the principle laid down in clause I of the Consti-

tutions that disputes as to advowsons and presenta-
tions (always classed as property in England) were to
be dealt with in the king's court, and in clause IX that
the decision whether land was held in free alms or as
a fief was to be a matter for the lay court (though
possibly the exact method prescribed, later known
as the *Assize Utrum*, was novel); similar, too, is
the question of debts, which by clause XV were to
be settled in the king's court, whether a definite
pledge had been entered into or not. We have no
information, so far as I know, as to how these questions
had been treated previously; the strong presumption certainly is that in these three cases, as in
the first six, Henry was correctly stating the former
practice.

This brings us to clause III, the crucial point at
issue between Henry II and Becket, and here I think
that Henry was possibly claiming even less than the
practice of his grandfather. William I and William II,
with Lanfranc's approval, had asserted their right to
sit in judgment on bishops Odo of Bayeux and William
of Durham, distinguishing between the temporal and
the spiritual functions of the bishop. A distinction of
a similar kind is implied in the first part of clause III.
Further, it is quite clear that, until Becket intervened,
clerks were being tried for criminal offences in the
king's courts; I see no reason to believe that this was
an innovation suddenly introduced by Henry II. On
this point Henry gave way, but he insisted on his
courts taking cognisance of the case and inflicting on
a degraded clerk the punishment any other layman
would have to suffer. It was this double punishment

which Becket resisted, repeating from canon law the familiar quotation out of Jerome's commentary on Nahum.[1] I do not want to traverse again ground that has been so well covered by Maitland, but it is necessary to point out that this was a vexed question, on which the ecclesiastical lawyers had not made up their minds. Professor Génestal has pointed out[2] that the practice condemned by Becket continued in France into the thirteenth century. And Pope Alexander III had written a *Summa* on the *Decretum*, before he became Pope, in which he seems to justify the double punishment.[3] As Pope he had no option but to uphold the principle for which Becket fought, and he later issued a decretal to this effect. It would seem that Becket was responsible for this decision in canon law,[4] which, as Maitland has shown, was in certain respects reversed later on by Pope Innocent III.

My view, then, is that Henry, regarding the reign of Stephen as a period of anarchy, naturally wished for a return of the old regime, and that in the Constitu-

[1] "Non iudicat Deus bis in idipsum." This is quoted in a canon of the Council of Mainz in 847 (reading, as Jerome, *vindicat* for *iudicat*), which is repeated in the Council of Worms in 868, and in several collections of ecclesiastical law (where, however, *iudicat* becomes the regular reading): Regino of Prum, Burchard, the *Tripartita*, Ivo's *Decretum* and *Pannormia*, and finally Gratian (C. xiii, qu. 2, cap. 30). As he reads *iudicat*, Becket probably was quoting from canon law and not directly from Jerome; though *vindicat* would have been much more suitable for his purpose.

[2] Génestal, R., *Le Privilegium Fori en France du décret de Gratien à la fin du xive siècle* (Bibl. de l'école des hautes études. Sciences religieuses, vols. XXXV, XXXIX. Paris, 1921, 24), vol. II, pp. 115 foll.

[3] *Summa Magistri Rolandi* (ed. Thaner, F.), Causa xi, quaestio 1.

[4] Génestal, R., *Thomas Becket et la Décretale At si clerici (c. 4. X.* II. 1) (Actes du Congrès international d'histoire des religions tenu à Paris en Octobre 1923, vol. II, pp. 330–343. Paris, 1925). This is repeated again in the same author's *Le Privilegium Fori*, vol. II.

tions of Clarendon he gave what is on the whole an accurate description of the customary practice in his grandfather's reign, erring, if anything, on the side of moderation.[1] The hand of Henry I had been heavy upon the Church, and the concessions in Stephen's charter suggest that the Church had had a great deal more to complain of than the customs Henry II sought to revive. Moreover, if he had been introducing novelties under the guise of customs, what an admirable argument his opponents would have had to use against him. But nobody in England seems to have questioned the fact that the Constitutions did represent the older practice. The controversy turned not on whether they were customs, but on whether they were right customs.

On the other hand, I think that Henry II committed a fatal blunder in publishing the Constitutions, which was a novelty. His predecessors had excluded papal authority simply by preventing certain things from happening; and without the aid of papal authority the bishops had not the inclination or the power to resist the royal control and the royal will in the matter of the secular and the ecclesiastical courts. But when these customs are written down as law to be obeyed, the bishops are immediately forced into a position in which they have to make public profession of choice between the law of the Church and the law of the State. It put them in an awkward dilemma. It also created a situation of which the Pope was forced to take cognisance. To say that the most vital rules of

[1] Cf. Pollock and Maitland, *History of English Law*, vol. I, 2nd ed., p. 452.

canon law, such as the right of every one to appeal to
Rome, and the duty of all bishops to visit the Pope,
were illegal, could not be overlooked. Previously it
had been a question of negotiation with the king, and
the attempt by diplomatic measures to soften the
king's resolution. Now there could be no harmony
until the obnoxious Constitutions had been with-
drawn, and the law of the Church recognised.

An illuminating commentary on this and other
aspects of the situation is provided in a letter[1] written
by Nicholas of Mont Saint-Jacques near Rouen to
Becket, describing a visit he had paid to Henry II's
mother, the Empress Matilda, at Christmas 1164 to
persuade her to use her influence with her son. He
was only partially successful, for the Empress was in
favour of some of the Constitutions, particularly of the
clause forbidding the king's servants to be excommunicated without royal licence. "The woman is of
the race of the tyrants", commented Nicholas. But of
some she did disapprove, and in particular she condemned their publication, since this necessitated the
bishops making a promise to observe them, which had
not been done before. Her proposal was that peace
should be brought about by a tacit understanding that
the ancient customs of the country should be observed,
though nothing was to be written down and no
promises extorted; the secular courts were to respect
the freedom of the Church, and the bishops were not
to abuse it. This suggestion was similar to the one
later made to Becket that he should promise to observe

[1] *Materials for the history of Archbishop Thomas Becket*, ed.
Robertson, J. C., Rolls Series, vol. v, pp. 144 foll.

the usages which had been preserved towards former kings by his predecessors. But the publication of the Constitutions made both these proposals impracticable; there could be no tacit understanding to observe what had been publicly condemned by the Pope. Matilda went on to call attention to abuses in the Church—the laxity about ordination, which led to many clergy being ordained uncanonically without a title and so attracted into crime by idleness and poverty, and the holding of pluralities, for which the bishops who endowed their relatives were as much to blame as the laity who rewarded their servants. Nicholas passed on these criticisms to Becket, himself once a notorious pluralist, and ventured humbly to suggest that if he loved the freedom of the Church he should set his face against these abuses. This was good advice, as but for offences within the Church the question of criminous clergy would not have arisen. But Becket's mind was too much set on offences against the Church to be able to consider offences within it.

Hitherto Becket had been engaged in living up to his conception of an archbishop, jealously contesting his rights and privileges and the authority of his courts; the question of the criminous clergy was still the chief cause of contention between him and the king. But when the king's hand became heavier and deliberately oppressive, he escaped to France and appealed to the Pope, to whom he showed the Constitutions. Henceforward it is not so much the rights of the archbishop as the rights of the Pope that matter;

the Pope condemned ten of the Constitutions, and we hear now much less about the issue between the secular and the ecclesiastical courts. The greater questions—the exclusion of papal authority from England—become much more important, especially the question of appeals; if these were not allowed, the whole machinery of ecclesiastical jurisdiction was thrown out of gear. And Henry did his best to prevent them, by the issue of ordinances and by a careful watch on the Channel ports. Becket accepted the change without hesitation, and became the champion of the larger issue between secular and ecclesiastical authority in general. He studied the law in his retirement at Pontigny, and quoted from it in his letters and manifestos, repeating especially the pronouncements of Gregory VII on this question. So there could be no peace, no reconciliation, so long as there was any word of the Constitutions or any suggestion of a pledge to observe the customs. To obtain a reconciliation, Henry eventually had to give way completely.

Becket would seem to have been more zealous in the Pope's cause, as well as his own, than the Pope himself. The freedom of the English Church, he repeats again and again, means freedom to obey the Pope, to be under papal government as the rest of the Church was; he is fighting not only the battle of the English Church, but of the whole Church and of the Pope. This was certainly the case, and therefore the Pope seems singularly backward in supporting him. But actually the publication of the Constitutions and the attitude of Becket were gravely embarrassing

to him. He was in the crisis of his contest with the
Emperor, and this absorbed all his interest. On the
other hand, he could not avoid taking cognisance of
the Constitutions, and he had no alternative but to
condemn most of them as contrary to the law of the
Church. Becket saw everything out of proportion. He
was concerned with the freedom of the Church in one
country, and that not the most important to the
Papacy; the Pope was defending the independence of
the Papacy itself. Ideally, perhaps, the Pope should
have acted as Becket wished, though this would have
meant that the two most powerful sovereigns in
Europe would have been allied against him. Practically, this would have been a fatal policy to pursue; so,
while firm on essentials, he was careful to do what he
could to placate Henry in minor matters. Becket
could make no distinction: questions into which
royal control did not enter, such as the granting of the
papal legation to the archbishop of York, the professions of obedience of the bishop of London and the
abbot of St Augustine's, the coronation of the young
Henry, were all major issues to him, because they
affected the prerogatives of Canterbury. He complained bitterly of the papal lethargy. He had another,
and much more legitimate, grievance—that Henry's
money enabled him to obtain adherents within the
papal Curia.

However, as the danger from the Empire receded,
the Pope was able to take a firmer line, and eventually
the reconciliation of Henry and Becket came about.
There was no word of customs or Constitutions, and
this meant a great victory for the freedom of the

Church. But Becket was not satisfied with that. He was determined to recover all the possessions of his church, and also to punish those who had taken part in the coronation of the young Henry. And it was his fierce vindication of the rights of Canterbury that was really responsible for his murder. That in the last days he expected his death seems certain, and he played his final rôle superbly and left an imperishable memory behind him. Everything he had done had been on the grand scale; lofty as was his conception of the parts he had to play, his performance was equal to his conception. He occupied the centre of the stage during the best part of his life, and he changed the course of English history. One can understand the devotion of his admirers, and also the antagonism of his opponents; his utterances arouse irritation when read at this distance of time. He was so self-centred that he would often sacrifice the prospect of an advantage in order to gain the ephemeral satisfaction of a verbal victory. As archbishop, except perhaps at the very beginning and at the very end, there is little in him of the spiritually minded man. Henry was noted for his violent temper, but he was often superior to Becket in patience and self-restraint, and he behaved really admirably at the time of the reconciliation; he showed far better grace in his defeat than Becket in his success.

Becket won a victory in his lifetime that might or might not have been lasting. But by his death he won a much more striking victory for the freedom of the Church, which was a permanent one; it was a victory,

14-2

however, rather for the Pope than for the archbishop.
The clause about criminous clerks was repealed,
though not apparently the other clauses affecting the
ecclesiastical courts. But Henry also promised to
allow freedom of appeals for the future, which meant
the discarding of the old barriers between England
and Rome, and therefore the nullification of the main
purpose of the Constitutions. And the effect of this
was equally striking in its positive as in its negative
results. I have already discussed this question at some
length,[1] and here I only wish to summarise briefly
what I then wrote. In one or two places that article
needs some verbal corrections, because three years
ago I had no idea of the amount or the character of
the ecclesiastical law that was current in England in
the twelfth century; but my conclusions remain
substantially the same. As a result of the concessions
of Henry II, canon law becomes at last completely
valid in this country; in the full practice of the law the
English Church is able to take its place with the rest
of the Church. Neither the knowledge nor the desire
had been lacking before, but only the power. The
king's authority had stood in the way. Now he with-
draws his opposition and allows free intercourse between Rome and England, and the working of the
law is able to take its normal course. There had been
an approximation to this in the reign of Stephen, but
only an approximation, as I have already shown.

The change after the death of Becket is especially
illustrated in the canon law itself. For in the

[1] In *The effects of Becket's murder on papal authority in England*
(Cambridge Historical Journal, vol. II, pp. 213–228).

Decretales of Gregory IX are included over 400 decretals of Alexander III, and the remarkable thing about them is that he addressed to this country more decretals than to all the rest of Europe put together. I made, in the article mentioned above, an analysis of them and of the points on which particular instruction was given to Englishmen. These decretals of Alexander III to England reveal a number of important facts: that appeals from England at once became numerous and regular as in other countries; that English bishops were applying to the Pope for advice on numerous points of canon law; that Englishmen were entering into the study of canon law with an enthusiasm unknown before, and were showing themselves especially zealous in the collection of papal decretals, particularly the recent ones;[1] and, finally, that the Pope was taking advantage of the cases coming from England to give solemn judgments on points which were either not dealt with in the law or were not decided definitely by papal authority. Even Gratian had left a number of points rather indecisive, and there was no complete code of law, procedure, and jurisprudence; a great deal that was customary was not written down, and the Roman customs had to be explained and enforced. This was particularly necessary in the case of England, and of course the

[1] The work that Professor W. Holtzmann is carrying out in his investigation of English libraries for all MSS. of papal letters, etc., shows the numbers of such documents which were collected in the latter part of the twelfth century. See his *Papsturkunden in England*, two parts of which have appeared as vol. xxv of the Abhandlungen der Gesell. d. Wissensch. z. Göttingen in 1930–1. Another point is the important part played by Englishmen in the formation of the *Compilationes* of decretals, prior to Gregory IX's authoritative collection.

majority of these decretals are concerned with questions of jurisdiction. The number of Alexander's
decretals to England is especially accounted for by the
need of instructing a part of the Church which up till
then had not been experienced in the full practice of
the law as worked at Rome. To take one instance to
show what I mean. Enormous readjustments were
required when appeals to Rome became lawful and
common. The bishop's court became much less important, and so did his functions as judge ordinary;
on the other hand, he commonly had to act on papal
instructions as judge delegate. This was a new field of
practice, the details of which had to be carefully
elaborated, and thirteen[1] of Alexander's decretals to
England deal with this topic. The point, then, is that
now at last we can see the canon law in full working
order in England, and therefore the normal exercise
of papal authority. This does not mean that the royal
authority was of no effect in the Church, or that all the
rules of canon law were implicitly adhered to. The
king exercised a very considerable control in certain
respects, and in the clash of legislations and jurisdictions the secular often won a victory over the
ecclesiastical. But this was the case in every country
in Europe. The papal authority and the canon law
have the same validity and the same efficacy in England as elsewhere, but the boundaries between the
two authorities could never be accurately defined, so
that disputes were bound to occur everywhere.

[1] Or seventeen, if we take into account the decretals in the *Compilationes* which were not included in the *Decretales*. As against
these seventeen to England, there were in all only five decretals of
Alexander III on this topic addressed to other countries.

CHAPTER XIV

EPILOGUE. FROM THE DEATH OF BECKET TO MAGNA CARTA

THE point at which the English Church falls into line with the rest of the Church in respect of obedience to Rome and the full working of the canon law of the Roman Church forms the natural *terminus ad quem* of the story which I have been tracing. But it is necessary to review the history of the next thirty or forty years in the light of the conclusions reached in the last chapter, in order to see whether the events of those years show the victory of the Papacy to have been a definite one, whether the position it had won was maintained. Farther than John's surrender to the Pope it is obviously not necessary to go, but up to that point there is a certain ambiguity in the situation which needs briefly to be elucidated.

The terms on which Henry was reconciled with the Church at Avranches in 1172 are told us, in identical language, by the king himself and by the papal legates.[1] He promised: (1) To maintain 200 knights at Jerusalem. (2) To allow freedom of appeals to Rome; if he was suspicious of an appellant, he might exact a pledge from him that he was planning no injury to king or kingdom. This saving clause did not, as some people have suggested, make the concession nugatory; we have seen that appeals at once became numerous, and with what result. (3) To repeal all the customs made in his own lifetime against the churches of his

---

[1] *Materials for...Becket*, vol. VII, pp. 518–522.

land. This was a promise he could easily give, for, as he adds himself, "paucas aut nullas aestimo"; this had always been his contention.[1] (4) To restore all the possessions of Canterbury and of Becket's fellow-exiles. Henry writes from Avranches, the legates from Caen, where they say that he publicly repeated his concessions before a more numerous assembly, and that he also released the bishops from the pledge they had given him to observe the customs and promised not to exact it in future. This seems undoubtedly correct, for we hear nothing more of the Constitutions. On the other hand, he continued many of his earlier practices. He had removed the former impediments to papal authority, but he maintained, so far as he could, his own control in the domestic affairs of the English Church, in particular over elections. These still seem to have taken place in the king's chamber, for Alexander III wrote a strong letter of rebuke to archbishop Richard on this very point. The king, despite his promise in 1173 of *libera electio* (which perhaps he limited to the sees then vacant), continued to appoint to the chief offices in the Church, and Richard and John were just as insistent on their rights in this respect. Canonical regulations were observed in form; the practice was, as before, not unlike the modern *congé d'élire*. The king also continued to administer the revenues of vacant sees, though he had to be content with short vacancies. And the familiar

---

[1] Dr Else Gütschow (*Innocent III und England*, pp. 188 foll.), ignoring this contention of Henry, argues that *consuetudines* here cannot refer to the "customs" but merely to monetary exactions. The statement of the legates from Caen clearly disproves her view.

story of his quarrel with Hugh of Lincoln shows that he would not tolerate his servants being excommunicated without his sanction. His control, however, was not so complete as it had been. We read that archbishop Richard on his election took the oath of fealty with a saving clause, and there is no word of homage. Also the mention of disputed elections, which were referred to the Pope for his decision, is another sign of limitation.

There is nothing peculiar to England in the exercise of royal control of this character. The Pope might contest its lawfulness, but he had to do so in other countries besides England. On the main questions— freedom of intercourse with Rome, and the normal working of Church law and ecclesiastical jurisdiction —there is no longer any difference between England and the Continent. On one point only did the English kings claim something peculiar to themselves, but they claimed it as a custom conceded by former Popes—that papal legates must obtain the king's consent before entering the country. They no longer excluded papal letters, but they were anxious to prevent a legate *a latere* from acting without their cognisance. This appears to be similar to the privilege granted to the Norman rulers of Sicily. But there is one difference. In England there were actually papal legates residing in the country, and though they were English bishops they certainly did take their orders from the Pope and acted by virtue of the authority they received from him.

There were four such papal legates during the last quarter of the twelfth century, the three archbishops of Canterbury—Richard, Baldwin, and Hubert Walter—and William Longchamp, bishop of Ely. There is no evidence that in any of these cases (except Longchamp, who, however, did not act as legate after Clement III's death) the office was renewed by the successor of the Pope who granted it;[1] the Pope therefore retained the initiative, and the archbishops of Canterbury were not yet *legati nati*, but had to receive definite appointment. All four held legatine visitations, and, with the exception of Baldwin, we have record that they all visited the province of York and also held a legatine council at Westminster; in the case of Richard and Hubert Walter the canons have been preserved to us.

There can be little doubt that Richard acted in close co-operation with the Pope. He both wrote to consult him on matters of ecclesiastical law and received from him a number of decretals, either as answers to his own questions or as decisions arising out of cases that had come from England to Rome. Some of these decretals of Alexander seem to be echoed in the canons of the Council which Richard held in 1175.[2] The subject-matter is the same in a number of cases; moreover, in one case Richard actually quotes a decretal letter of Alexander to the bishop of Norwich and in another case also invokes Alexander's authority. There were causes of friction,

[1] Cf. Tillmann, H., *Die päpstlichen Legaten in England*, p. 34, though in some respects her information about these archbishops is incomplete.

[2] E. Seckel (*Die Westminster-Synode*, 1175, Deutsche Zeitschrift für Kirchenrecht, 3 Folge, vol. IX, p. 177) considers that some of the canons of this Council were wrongly attributed as decretals to Alexander III in the *Compilationes*.

too. Alexander severely blamed Richard for allowing elections of bishops to take place in the king's chamber. On the other hand, the archbishop wrote to protest about exemptions of monasteries from episcopal jurisdiction. These were becoming much more numerous, in England and elsewhere, and undoubtedly the Papacy favoured the policy, for its influence was thereby increased. So Richard protested in vain. But the delegated authority from the Pope made it possible for him to visit all monasteries, exempt or otherwise, and he dealt severely with the numerous cases of laxity which he discovered.

Richard also was well read in the canon law. In his Council of 1175 he quoted canonical authority, like Lanfranc in 1075, for almost all the decrees that he promulgated, deriving it in most cases from Gratian. And we possess a letter written by him to three other English bishops (three of Becket's former opponents) which contains a number of references to canon law. The letter[1] is so interesting that it deserves a digression. Richard is angrily deploring the fact that laymen who murder an ecclesiastic are punishable with excommunication only, which has no deterrent effect, and are not put to death. The theft of a sheep or a goat is treated more severely than the murder of a clerk. The fault, he says, lies with ourselves, because we insist on the cases being dealt with in the ecclesiastical courts, though the king is most anxious to punish the offenders. What actually happens is that the criminals go to Rome and there obtain

[1] *Materials for the history of Archbishop Thomas Becket*, ed. Robertson, J. C., Rolls Series, vol. VII, pp. 561 foll.

absolution; he instances a case that has recently occurred at Winchester. He quotes several authorities from canon law (probably again from Gratian) to show that the secular sword may be called in when the ecclesiastical jurisdiction needs supplementing. Further, he argues that this would not mean that the prisoner would be punished twice for the same offence, for there is no duplication where what is begun by one is completed by another.[1] This is strange doctrine for the successor of St Thomas. He makes no reference to the question of criminous clerks; in their case he would doubtless have argued that degradation made the matter "complete" and constituted an adequate punishment. He is careful to refer to the canon of the Council of Mainz about condemned criminals,[2] and to explain that in their case the refusal of the sacraments of the Church would mean a double penalty. Altogether it is an instructive letter, for though the argument is logical and orthodox, it reveals the dilemma which Becket's doctrine had created, and provides considerable justification for Henry's anxiety on behalf of law and order.

Of his successor Baldwin as legate we know no more than that he held a legatine visitation. He was soon on bad terms with the Pope owing to his quarrel with his monks; but in earlier days, as abbot of Ford,

---

[1] There is considerable ambiguity in his language, but I do not think that Pollock and Maitland (*History of English Law*, vol. I, 2nd ed., p. 457) are right in inferring that he is advocating the double punishment of excommunication followed by execution. His wish seems to be that the offenders, after being found guilty in the ecclesiastical courts, instead of being excommunicated should be handed over to the lay power for punishment.

[2] See above, p. 205, n. I.

he had certainly enjoyed the confidence of Alexander III. The other two legates belong to Richard's reign, when the situation was complicated by two factors—the absence of the king from England and the temporary weakness of the Papacy. Richard was just as determined as his father to retain the control of appointments in his own hands. But he did what Henry II had planned to do in the case of Becket, and had then determined not to do again; he united the chief secular and ecclesiastical offices in the same hands. Sheriffdoms were bought by bishops, and the office of justiciar, especially important when the king was regularly absent, was held both by Longchamp and Hubert Walter together with the office of papal legate. They therefore were the representatives of the executive powers of both king and Pope in this country. By Longchamp, able as he undoubtedly was, the two powers were used as a joint instrument of authority, much as Wolsey used them in the sixteenth century. In the case of Hubert Walter there is more distinction, and the canons of his legatine council of Westminster, as I have shown, mark a complete recognition of his subordination to the Pope. And though both of these capable men could act up to a point without impediment, in the sequel there is also a striking difference. It was a conspiracy against Richard's government that caused Longchamp's fall; but it was the Pope, Innocent III, who insisted on Hubert renouncing the justiciarship and confining himself to his ecclesiastical duties. Hubert Walter did, indeed, later become chancellor, but he no longer held legatine authority.

The history of the Papacy from Alexander III to
Innocent III[1] is marked by what at first appears as a
strange decline after its triumph over Frederick Barbarossa. But Frederick had shown great skill and tact
in conciliating opinion to himself in Italy, and his
position was much enhanced by the betrothal of his
son Henry VI to the heiress of the Sicilian kingdom.
Henry VI was more powerful in Italy during his short
reign than any Emperor had been. Accordingly the
Curia was content merely to mark time and to await
events, but always ready to take the initiative when
occasion offered. For in the seventeen years between
Alexander III's death and Innocent III's accession
there were five Popes, all old men, and so vacancies
were frequent. In other ways, too, the Curia seems to
show, even in opposition to the Pope, its reluctance to
adopt a forward policy. But the death of Henry VI,
shortly followed by that of Pope Celestine III, gave
the opportunity, and the election of the youngest and
most vigorous of the cardinals as Pope Innocent III
brought about an entire change. So this is not a
period satisfactory to test the working of the new
system, for nowhere did the Papacy effectively assert
itself. Yet its claims remained undiminished, and were
in fact gradually extending. Innocent III, in his
references to the plenitude of papal power, was only
repeating what his immediate predecessors had said,[2]

---

[1] Cf. Wenck, Karl, *Die römischen Päpste zwischen Alexander III
und Innocenz III und der Designationsversuch Weihnachten* 1197.

[2] In letters addressed to England alone I have found the phrase
used, exactly in the way Innocent III used it later on, by Alexander
III (Jaffé-Löwenfeld, 11917), Lucius III (*ib.* 15164), and Celestine
III (*ib.* 17202).

though he more definitely translated the claim into action; he was also only copying what his predecessors did when he asserted his right to appoint to benefices and prebends and even to reserve such appointments for himself.[1] There is resistance in England, as elsewhere; but the fullness of the papal power is not questioned, though the particular exercise of it may often be challenged.

There is record both of appeals to Rome and of letters to the Pope asking for his decision on points of law; but the instances are few. It is not possible to infer any change from this, because papal decretals to England were so much less numerous; it was mainly the abnormal number of Alexander III's decretals that had shown how numerous appeals were in his time. On the other hand, there were a number of *causes célèbres* in this period, all of which were referred to Rome. There was the question of archbishop Geoffrey of York, Henry II's illegitimate son, who eventually had to retire to France, mainly for political reasons. There were also a number of protracted disputes between monasteries and bishops—Evesham and Worcester, Glastonbury and Bath, above all Christ Church, Canterbury, and its archbishop. These, perhaps, were all greater cases which might have gone to Rome at any time during our period. But I very much doubt whether they would have arisen at all in

[1] E.g. Alexander III (Jaffé-Löwenfeld, 11917) and Celestine III (*ib.* 17618); again I am only giving English instances. Notice (1) that in the earliest cases in which Innocent III claims this right, he is almost always confirming an act of Celestine III; (2) that his most frequent allusions to *plenitudo potestatis* are in connection with this right of appointment. This is also the case with Alexander III in the instance quoted in this and the preceding note.

earlier times. It was the exercise of papal authority which had encouraged monastic independence, against which Lanfranc had set his face; the king, too, would then have prevented the internal strife which is so marked at this time. At any rate, though the evidence is slight for this period, I can see no signs of a reaction to the earlier system, or any attempt to prevent free intercourse between England and Rome.

One of these internal conflicts is so important, particularly in its results, that it needs special consideration—that of archbishops Baldwin and Hubert Walter with the monks of their cathedral church of Christ Church, the correspondence about which fills a volume in the Rolls Series, edited by Stubbs, who has given a detailed account of the contest in his introduction. The archbishop wished to set up a house for secular canons, and for this purpose to revoke some of the lavish grants made to the monks by his predecessors. The monks naturally contested their loss of property, but they were equally if not more determined against the secular canons. They felt that their own rights in the election of the archbishop were endangered, and probably this was the intention; for Baldwin assigned stalls to his suffragan bishops in his new foundation. The great issue then is the election of the archbishop. The monks had repeatedly asserted their right to elect the archbishop, who was also their abbot; there is an echo of this in earlier times in the stress they lay on the appointment of a regular. They had a second basis of claim, since they formed the chapter of the cathedral; and at each vacancy they seem to have been successful in getting their right to a share in the election recognised. But only to a share. For by custom the suffragan bishops of Canterbury had also a share in the election of the archbishop; on the Continent the sole right of the chapter to elect had become the universal rule. There is no doubt that this English custom was most irksome to the Canterbury monks. No monastery was so jealous of its privileges, and monastic privileges in general, as Christ Church.[1] They were now faced with the danger that they might be deprived of any share in the election at all.

The earnestness of the monks in this long struggle with the two archbishops is shown by the persecution they endured, and by their constant appeals to Rome; they kept some of their number continually in residence at Rome to prosecute their case, and several of them actually died there. The Papacy took their side, but the determined efforts of the archbishops supported by the king availed to delay a definitive decision, until the accession of Innocent III, who was resolute to bring the matter to a speedy conclusion. The archbishop was compelled to pull down the obnoxious foundation, and the immediate danger to the monks was removed. But not their fears. And so, when Hubert Walter died, they hastily elected one of their number and sent him to Rome for papal confirmation. The king was furious, as were the bishops whose rights had been evaded; they could not now avoid a papal decision on the matter, and they tried to get it in their favour by sending a candidate of their own. Innocent again upheld the monks, but he quashed their election as irregular, and induced them to elect

[1] See above, chapter VIII, pp. 123–125.

instead the English cardinal, Stephen Langton. Thus began the great conflict between king and Pope which was to end in John's complete submission. On the question of the election of the archbishop of Canterbury, in which the king's will had hitherto prevailed, he was now decisively defeated by the Pope. And in Magna Carta his first promise is to allow freedom of election to the English Church.

This is not the end of the story, but I have reached the limit I set myself when I started to consider the relations of the English Church with the Papacy. My object was to discover exactly what the facts were, and I have been able at any rate to clear up my own mind on the subject. It is difficult to approach such an issue, or indeed any great historical issue, without some measure of prejudice, or at least without some preconceived idea of what the result is likely to be. In my own case I must confess that I started with a vague idea which I have had to discard. I had already come to the conclusion that the English Church fell into line with the rest of the Church in the latter part of the twelfth century, but it did appear before that to be tending towards independence and taking a distinct course of its own. This was only a hazy idea, because one had to view it through the mists of contradictory hypotheses. I have tried to discover the facts behind the mists, and what I have discovered has changed my point of view completely. As I now see it, the English Church was in mind at one with the Church as a whole throughout the period. It moved along the same path, more slowly indeed than was usually the case elsewhere, but always in the same direction. Everywhere the monarchy and the episcopate began by opposing, from perfectly sincere motives as well as from self-interest, the new centralising policy of the Papacy. Everywhere they were forced to accept it, the bishops first, because conviction gradually came to them from the study of the law and the authorities they all revered; the kings later, as circumstances forced them, most reluctantly, to yield. But they too in time came to the same general acceptance. This happened very quickly in France, where the reform movement had its origin, and where the royal power was weak. It was slowest in Germany, where the tradition of obedience to the king was strongest, and where the imperial authority could rely on the precedents of centuries not merely for its control over the national Church but over the Papacy as well. England occupies a mean position. The episcopate absorbed the new ideas more slowly than in France, but the king was forced to yield to circumstances sooner than in Germany. Yet from the beginning there was no intention in the English Church to be distinct. When the realisation came to the bishops that they were tending to become so, that the Pope was justified in his claims, many of them did their best to change direction and to become one with the rest of the Church. This, we have seen, is the meaning in the demand for the "freedom of the Church" from the time of Stephen onwards. Henry II attempted to restore the former state of affairs, but was firmly resisted by Becket, though on an issue between the lay

15-2

and ecclesiastical courts which was really independent
of the main question. The main issue was joined when
the Constitutions of Clarendon were published, and
was decided, as a result of Becket's murder, by the
king's surrender in 1172. Previously the king had
insisted that all intercourse between England and the
Pope must be conducted through himself alone; now
he allows free intercourse, which means the normal
working of the canon law and of ecclesiastical jurisdiction. The king did not thereby relinquish all
authority over the Church and its officials, especially
over their appointments, nor did he leave the ecclesiastical courts free to administer those rules of canon
law which ran counter to the law of the land. It is
easy to point to cases where the Church was over-
ridden by the State, but exceptions must not blind us
to the general rule. Here again, a knowledge of
general Church history enables us to see things in
their right proportion. In no country did the Church
obtain all that it demanded. Different problems arose,
varying from country to country but similar in character, owing to the conflicting claims of the two laws.
The thirteenth century sees papal authority at the
zenith, and its encroachments on the secular domain
are as marked in England as elsewhere; while, when
the reaction came at the end of the century, it was far
more violent and extensive in France than in England.

I have confined myself to the purely historical
aspect of this question, to discover what did happen
and why it happened. Into the rights and wrongs of
the matter I have not entered, for that would lead me
into the well-worn theme of the *sacerdotium* and the

regnum. Nor do I regard it as a question of right and wrong. Selfish interests and individual ambitions often entered in, but behind lay a clash of ideals, a conflict of two opposing rights. Between them I have no desire to arbitrate. It seems to me far more important to understand than to judge. What will be universally acknowledged is that, by this conflict, the history of England, especially in its constitutional development, has been profoundly affected. For a right understanding of this, it is necessary first to be clear as to the relations between the two powers and the inclination to either side of the local ecclesiastical authorities; and therefore it is essential to decide what was the validity of the papal authority and Roman canon law in England. It is on this subject that I have attempted in the preceding pages to describe both my conclusions and how I arrived at them, and in the light of those conclusions to display the main current of English Church history in the eleventh and twelfth centuries.

APPENDIX

ENGLISH MANUSCRIPTS CONTAINING COLLECTIONS OF ECCLESIASTICAL LAW

(See Chapters V *and* VI)

CHAPTER V

LANFRANC'S COLLECTION

(a) COMPLETE COPIES

MS.	Date	Provenance
1. Trinity Coll. Camb. 405 (B. 16. 44).	xi cent.	Canterbury
2. Peterhouse, 74.	xi–xii cent.	Durham
3. Corpus Christi Coll. Camb. 130.	xi–xii cent.	
4. B.M. Cotton. Claud. D. ix.	xi–xii cent.	
5. Hereford Cath. Lib. O. 8. viii.	xi–xii cent.	Hereford
6. Hereford Cath. Lib. O. 4. v. ⎱ P. 2. viii. ⎰	xii cent.	Hereford
7. Salisbury Cath. Lib. 78.	xi–xii cent.	Salisbury
8. B.M. Royal, 9. B. xii.	early xii cent.	Worcester
9. Lincoln Cath. Lib. 161.	xii cent.	Lincoln
10. B.M. Royal, 11. D. viii.	xii cent.	Gloucester Abbey
*11. Paris, Bibl. Nat. Latin, 1563.	xv cent.	

(b) DECRETALS ONLY

*12. Rouen, 701.	xii cent.	Jumièges
*13. Rouen, 703 (defective at end).	xii cent.	Jumièges
*14. Paris, Bibl. Nat. Latin, 3856.	xii cent.	Normandy

(c) COUNCILS ONLY

15. Oxford. Bodl. 810.	xii cent.	Exeter

* These four MSS. are added for the sake of completeness. Though they are not English MSS., I think they all derive ultimately from Lanfranc's copy.

(d) FRAGMENTS

MS.	Date	Provenance
16. Lincoln Cath. Lib. 106.	xi–xii cent.	

(Contains first four Ecumenical Councils and Regula Attici, preceded by Canones Apostolorum and a letter of Gregory I, enjoining obedience to the four Councils.)

17. Oxford Bodl. Rawlinson, A. 433.	xii cent.	Waltham Abbey

(Contains first three letters of Clement only.)

18. B.M. Harleian, 633.	xii cent.	

(Contains first three letters of Clement only.)

(e) A COLLECTION ABRIDGED FROM LANFRANC'S COL-LECTION (and followed by an abridgment of Gregory I's letters in 14 books).

19. Durham Cath. Lib. B. iv. 18.	xii cent.	Canterbury
20. Lambeth, 351.	xii cent.	

Nos. 16 to 20 have already been sufficiently described in the text. I want to say something further about the fifteen MSS. which contain one or both parts of this collection complete. I have already given my reasons for believing that Lanfranc's MS. is the parent of the whole group.

The material common to them all is (a) Decretals, 137 in all, concluding with the oath of Berengar in 1059; (b) Councils, from Canones Apostolorum to the Second Council of Seville. No. 1 (Lanfranc's own copy) also contains (1) the letter from Nicholas II to Lanfranc (Jaffé-Löwenfeld, 4446), at the end of the Decretals and in the same hand. At the end of the Councils, but in different hands, it contains (2) the letter from Alexander II to Lanfranc (J.L. 4669), and (3) the statement that "Ego Lanfrancus" bought this book from Bec and gave it to Christ Church. Subsequently were added (4) three letters from the anti-Pope Clement III to Lanfranc, and (5) three apocryphal canons in favour of monks.

Nos. 2 and 3 are very closely connected. They both contain, at the end of the Decretals and in the same hand, the letters of Nicholas II and Alexander II, with the marginal notes from Lanfranc's MS. (saying when he received them) pre-fixed as titles, and Gregory VII's Council of 1079 as far as the oath of Berengar, which is not in Lanfranc's MS.; after the Councils they both contain Lanfranc's letter "venerando Hiberniae episcopo D." (ep. 36). Otherwise they approximate closely to the original, and, to judge from the two additions to his MS. which they have in common, they probably derive from a copy made in Lanfranc's lifetime at Canterbury. They also both have additional material in different hands. In no. 2 there are a number of papal and other letters, the decrees of the First Lateran Council of 1123 (not 1133 as in the Catalogue), and the third apocryphal canon in favour of monks from the end of Lanfranc's MS. ("Oportet eos qui seculum reliquerunt...''), which is another sign of connection with Canterbury. The only important addition in no. 3 consists of the canons of the Council of 1143 (Wilkins, *Concilia*, vol. I, p. 417), which are wrongly ascribed by a later hand in the MS. (and in the Catalogue) to Gregory VII.

The French MSS. (nos. 11 to 14), which otherwise adhere closely to Lanfranc's original, all[1] add the 1079 Council with Berengar's oath, which is also added to the Salisbury MS. (no. 7). The other MSS. (nos. 4, 5, 6, 8, 9, 10) have no additions after the 1059 oath of Berengar. In only two of these eleven MSS. are there any additions at the end in later hands. No. 10 (from Gloucester) adds the decree of Paschal II's Council of 1112 against investiture. No. 12 (from Jumièges) has the canons of Innocent II's Council at Rheims in 1131, and the letter of Pope Alexander III to the archbishop of Canterbury (J.L. 13802).

Nos. 4 to 9 are obviously associated. They have a number of small variations from the text of Lanfranc's MS., e.g. the letter of Leo I "ad Aquiliensem episcopum" (Hinschius, p. 574) is by them addressed "ad Aquilienses episcopos"; in Urban I's letter (Hinschius, p. 143) the seven sections have

---

[1] Except no. 13, which ends in the middle of Gregory I's replies to Augustine's queries (Hinschius, p. 742, *ad init.*), the last folios being missing.

been numbered as six, because two have been joined together; the letter of Pope Felix (Hinschius, p. 484) ends "sententiam promere" instead of "promere sententiam"; in the decretal of Pope Hilary (Hinschius, p. 630) section 2 begins "Vel penitentes" instead of "Ut penitentes". Some, though not all, of the variants are also in no. 10. I venture the conjecture (a very tentative one) that no. 5 was the source of these variants, and was perhaps a copy sent round to a certain number of cathedrals as a pattern. It is now at Hereford, and at any rate I feel certain that no. 6 was copied from it. The MS. I call no. 6 consists of what are now two separate MSS., O. 4. v containing the Decretals and P. 2. viii the Councils. They are written in various twelfth-century hands, and together they form a faithful copy of no. 5. Apart from their peculiarly close agreement in the text with this older MS. in the same cathedral library, there are two other points leading to the same conclusion. A few passages of the Decretals in no. 5 are marked with a monogram of "Nota" in the margin; in each case this is copied in the margin of O. 4. v (a rather similar mark appears in the Worcester copy, no. 8). Secondly, there are two passages in P. 2. viii—caps. 67 and 68 of the Fourth Council of Toledo—where the scribe had omitted some words in the text and added them in the margin. In both cases his eye had obviously jumped from one "aecclesiae" to another "aecclesiae" a line or two lines immediately below. Now in O. 8. viii, which I take to be the MS. from which the scribe was copying, this condition is exactly fulfilled; he left out in one case exactly one line, in the other case exactly two lines, of his original. He must have been using this or another exactly similarly aligned copy. Both the MSS. which go to make up no. 6 are definitely Hereford Cathedral books. No. 5 is not so clearly of the same origin. Hence my conjecture in the text that it may have been sent or borrowed in order to be copied, and then not returned.

Nos. 2, 3, 12, 14, and 15 have copied the "a" mark which is in the margin of Lanfranc's MS. This seems again to bring those MSS. into close contact with the original. No. 2 is the most careful, and in it are marked most of the passages marked in Lanfranc's MS., and no others. The scribe or scribes of no. 3, who in other respects too were somewhat careless, have put in most of the marks but not always quite opposite the right passage. The two French MSS. have only a limited number of passages marked; they agree with Lanfranc's MS. at first but differ somewhat later on. In no. 5 (which is a copy of the Councils only) the marks have only been put in the latter part; where they occur, they agree with Lanfranc's MS. The "a" mark occurs also in no. 7 (the Salisbury MS.), several times on each page, as well as another mark "D.M." It looks as if somebody was proposing to compile an abridgment from this copy.

Finally, nos. 2 and 3 again imitate Lanfranc's MS. by copying from it the marginal note opposite one of the clauses of the *Capitula Ingilramni*. This is also copied in no. 9 (which otherwise has no marginalia) and in no. 7.

My general conclusion, as far as the English MSS. are concerned, is that, first, a faithful copy was made of Lanfranc's MS. at Canterbury at an early stage, when it ended at the declaration "Ego Lanfrancus" but already included the letters from Nicholas II and Alexander II; that to this copy, made perhaps under Lanfranc's eye, were added the extract from the 1079 Council and the letter of Lanfranc to the Irish bishop; and that from this, now lost, MS. the Peterhouse and Corpus MSS. (nos. 2 and 3) were copied. And that, secondly, another copy was made, also at an early date, from Lanfranc's MS. which excluded the letters of Nicholas II and Alexander II as not being canonical material, and that from this copy derive most, if not all, of the other English MSS.

CHAPTER VI

I. THE FALSE DECRETALS (UNABRIDGED).

(Ed. P. Hinschius, *Decretales Pseudo-Isidorianae*, Leipzig, 1863.)

(a) COMPLETE COPIES

MS.	Date	Provenance
1. Eton, 97.	xii cent.	
2. B.M. Royal, 11. D. iv.	xv cent.	

(Almost certainly a copy of the Eton MS.)

(b) DECRETALS ONLY

3. B.M. Cotton. Claud. E. v.	xii cent.	Canterbury
4. Camb. Univ. Dd. i. 10, 11.	xv cent.	

(Almost certainly a copy of the Cotton. MS.)

(c) DECRETALS followed by early General Councils only

5. Oxford Bodl. Hatton, 6.	xiii cent.

There are only two known twelfth-century copies (nos. 1 and 3). I described them sufficiently in the text, where I suggested that they both derive from Bec originals. I did not mention the Bodleian MS. (no. 5). It is really outside the scope of my enquiry, as it was written in the thirteenth century and in France. But it presents certain features of interest. It was in an English library in the fourteenth century, for as a title to the book "Canones Apostolorum" has been written at the top of the first page in a fourteenth-century English hand; the same title in a later hand has been pasted on to the binding at the back. The volume actually starts with the Canones Apostolorum. This illustrates the common practice in medieval libraries of describing a book by the first entry in it. In the catalogue of the Glastonbury library made in 1274 (Trin. Coll. Camb. MS. 724, ff. 102 foll.; printed in Hearne, T., *Joannis Glastoniensis*, vol. II, pp. 423 foll.), there is an entry among the books of canon law—"Canones apostolorum libri III cum quibusdam conciliis generalibus in primitiva ecclesia celebratis". This would do very well as a description of the Lincoln MS. 106 (no. 16 under Lanfranc's collection above); it might equally well apply to this Bodleian MS. In fact, in view of the mention of "libri III", it is more likely that it was a book of this kind, a complete collection of the False Decretals followed by early General Councils.

II. THE DECRETUM OF BURCHARD OF WORMS IN TWENTY BOOKS

(Printed first at Paris in 1549, and reprinted in Migne, PL. CXL.)

(a) COMPLETE COPIES

MS.	Date	Provenance
1. Durham Cath. Lib. B. iv. 17.	xii cent.	Durham
2. B.M. Cotton. Claud. C. vi.	xi cent.	?Canterbury

(b) FRAGMENT

3. St John's Coll. Oxford, 125.	xii cent.	

(c) AN ABRIDGMENT

4. Hereford Cath. Lib. O. 2. vii.	xii cent.	Hereford (probably)

Of the two complete copies, no. 1 agrees with Migne as far as the end of bk. XVIII. Bk. XIX, which is not separated from XVIII, is quite different from the text in Migne, though dealing with the same subject. Bk. XX again agrees with Migne, but some caps. are omitted. The MS. starts with a few letters of Ivo of Chartres; in consequence of this, it is headed "Decreta Yvonis", and it is so described in the medieval catalogues also. No. 2 is probably of foreign origin, but it may have come at an early date to Canterbury. The other material now bound up with it certainly comes from Canterbury, but unfortunately in the case of Cottonian MSS. fragments from different sources have often been bound together.

No. 3 is really a MS. of the *Pannormia* of Ivo of Chartres, which was written as far as the middle of cap. 37 of bk. VII, breaking off in the middle of f. 79, the rest of the page being

left blank. A new scribe started on f. 79ᵛ and wrote out bk. VII
of Burchard (the page-heading makes it appear as part of bk. VII
of the *Pannormia*) and bk. VIII as far as the middle of cap. 33
(headed, again, as bk. VIII of the *Pannormia*). Superficially
this MS. has the appearance of being a normal copy of the
Pannormia in eight books.

No. 4 consists of two independent compilations of canons,
bound up together, in both of which the principal ingredient
is an abstract of Burchard. It certainly seems to be an English
MS. in origin, and on the fly leaves are written in, at the
beginning the canons of the First Lateran Council, at the end
the canons of the Councils at Westminster held by Anselm in
1108, by John of Crema in 1125, and by archbishop William
in 1127. Part I begins (ff. 1–11) with extracts from Councils
followed mainly by extracts from the False Decretals, concluding with the words "Finit de corpore canonum". Folios 11–24
contain a mixed collection, which includes Peter Damiani's
"Sicut ad patrem familias" to Alexander II and Damasus I's
letter *de corepiscopis*. Folios 25–43 contain a short abridgment
from Burchard, canons being taken from all the books and
in the same order as in Burchard. This concludes with the
"sermo synodalis" and some canons of the Council at
Seligenstadt in 1022, both of which are also in Durham B. iv.
17. Folios 43 foll. contain various lists—that of Popes ending
with Urban II (Victor III being omitted). This, together with
the material added on the fly leaves, seems to suggest an early
twelfth-century date for this MS.

Part II (ff. 49–153) consists of an abridgment of Burchard
on a much larger scale, with a considerable number of additions, mainly from the False Decretals and Councils. As is
often the case, the compiler started off on an elaborate piece
of work but became much less ambitious as he went on. The
first three books are preceded by a table of contents, and on
some subjects such as simony a large number of extracts have
been collected from other sources. At one point in bk. I a
series of over 100 extracts from the False Decretals are inserted, from Clement to Melchiades in their correct order.

From bk. IV onwards there are no headings to the books or tables of contents, and the extracts are no longer numbered. The additions become fewer and fewer, and disappear after bk.VII. There are no extracts from bks.VI and XVIII of Burchard. In place of bk. XVIII there is a heading "Incipiunt capitula ex sanctorum patrum decretis", followed by 164 extracts, the first 119 without, the last 45 with attributions. These seem to be derived partly from the *Dionysio-Hadriana*, partly from the *Hispana* (cf. the Canterbury MS. in the next section). After this digression the compiler resumes with bk. XIX of Burchard down to "sceleris celandi faciat" in cap. 5 (Migne, col. 972). Then comes bk. XX complete, with its table of contents, heading, and all the 110 canons as in Burchard. Finally he returns to bk. XIX, cap. 6 and with a few omissions continues to the middle of cap. 32 where the MS. breaks off.

III. THE NEW ROMAN COLLECTIONS OF THE ELEVENTH CENTURY

(a) THE COLLECTION IN 74 TITLES

(This has not been printed, but it is fully described by P. Fournier in *Le premier manuel canonique de la réforme du XIe siècle*, École française de Rome. Mélanges d'archéologie et d'histoire, vol. XIV, pp. 147–223. Rome, 1894.)

MS.	Date	Provenance
1. Canterbury Cath. Lib. B. 7 (2).	xii cent.	Canterbury
2. B.M. Arundel, 173, ff. 79 foll.	xii cent.	
3. B.M. Add. 22,286, ff. 5 foll.	xii cent.	

The Canterbury MS., which is headed "Diversorum patrum sententiae de primatu Romanae ecclesiae", is composed of five books, the first three of which consist of a rearranged and enlarged edition of the *Collection in 74 titles*. The author seems to have carefully checked his references. He has occasionally corrected the addresses, e.g. correct addresses are given to caps. 27 and 28, and cap. 81 is taken from Marcellinus instead of from the *Capitula Ingilramni*. Also he sometimes adds to, or otherwise varies, the text of a passage. The first 11 titles (caps. 1–96) are copied in exact order. Afterwards there is considerable rearrangement and many additions. A few titles are omitted, a number of new ones added, and frequently two or more titles are joined into one. Only 17 caps. of the original collection are omitted; in four cases two caps. are joined into one; and 121 new caps. are added. As a result this collection in three books has 63 titles and 415 caps. in place of 74 titles and 315 caps. The new material is almost all from the False Decretals and Gregory I's letters, so that it is exactly the same in kind. The only two extracts from Councils in the original are excluded from this collection.

The fourth book consists almost entirely of Councils. There are a few extracts from early Councils, but the bulk of this book is filled up with the complete canons of certain Councils, which are not arranged in order of date. Among them are the Councils of Orange (529), Clermont (535), Orleans (538), Valence (855). Nicholas II's decretal letter from the Council of 1059 is given, and also Gregory VII's Council of November 1078, followed by two long decretals "de prava consuetudine" and "de ordinationibus", both attributed to Gregory VII, and a treatise "de loquela digitorum" without attribution.

Up to this point, this collection seems to resemble the Collection in 4 books mentioned by M. Fournier. The compiler has, however, added a fifth book of 120 canons, preceded by a table of *capitula*, which, like the extracts inserted in place of bk. XVIII of Burchard in the Hereford MS. mentioned in the last section, seem to be derived from the *Dionysio-Hadriana* together with the *Hispana*.[1] A few more extracts of a general character bring this MS. to an end.

The two British Museum MSS. which contain this

[1] As I have shown above (p. 91, n. 1), these 120 canons are actually part 1 of the collection known as the *Dacheriana*, while the 45 canons with attributions in the Hereford MS are abstracts from the three books of the *Dacheriana*. I have not been able to find the source of the 119 canons without attributions in the Hereford MS. Cf. Le Bras, G., *Les deux formes de la Dacheriana* in *Mélanges Paul Fournier*, pp. 395–414 (Paris, 1929).

collection are clearly of foreign origin. Add. 22,286 comes from the Bibl. Rosny and was not in England in the twelfth century, and the same is almost certainly true of Arundel 173 as well. They are headed "Plurimorum sanctorum sententiae de primatu Romanae ecclesiae". They are not complete copies, but abridgments; abridgments, however, not of the original *Collection in 74 titles* but of an enlarged and rearranged collection closely resembling the Canterbury MS. Except for a difference of arrangement in one place, they agree with the Canterbury MS. in most particulars; for instance, in attributions, such as that of cap. 81 to Marcellinus; and there are less than ten chapters in them which are not to be found in the Canterbury MS. Add. 22,286 is the shorter of the two and might well have been compiled from Arundel 173; with one possible exception I think there is nothing in it which is not in the Arundel MS.

(*b*) THE COLLECTIO CANONUM OF ANSELM OF LUCCA IN 13 BOOKS

> (This has never been printed in full. F. Thaner began an edition, of which two parts appeared at Innsbruck in 1906 and 1915. This goes down to bk. XI, cap. 15.)

MS.	Date	Provenance
1. Corpus Christi Coll. Camb. 269.	xii cent.	

This MS., unknown to Thaner, and previously regarded as a compilation from Ivo, is like all MSS. of Anselm written in an Italian hand. It has no heading, and the table of contents of the 13 books is different from that given by Thaner. In the tables of *capitula* before each book the gaps, a curious feature of MSS. of Anselm, are sometimes filled in, not always by the same hand. It is impossible to say when this MS. came into England. All that is definitely known about it is that it belonged in the fifteenth century to the Cistercian abbey of Pipewell, Northants. It is not likely that Anselm's collection would have been in any demand after the twelfth century and, therefore, as I suggested in the text, it is improbable that it travelled much after that date.

IV. COLLECTIONS OF ABSTRACTS

(a) ABRIDGMENT OF LANFRANC'S COLLECTION

(For MSS., see under Lanfranc's collection, nos. 19 and 20. I described them sufficiently in the text.)

(b) TRIPARTITA OR COLLECTIO TRIUM PARTIUM

(This has not been printed, but it has been fully described: pts. I and II by P. Fournier, *Les collections canoniques attribuées à Yves de Chartres*, Bibl. de l'école des chartes, vol. LVII, pp. 645 foll.; pt. III by H. Wasserschleben, *Beiträge zur Geschichte der vorgratianischen Kirchenrechtsquellen*, pp. 52 foll. Leipzig, 1839.)

MS.	Date	Provenance
1. Gonville and Caius Coll. xii cent.		
Camb. 455.		
2. Oxford. Bodl. d'Orville, 46. xii cent.		

The Caius MS. seems to be certainly English, the Oxford MS. is probably N. French. But the two are very similar, and in some respects differ from the MSS. described by Fournier and Wasserschleben, particularly in pt. III, the abridgment from Ivo's *Decretum*. There is no enumeration of books and caps.; it is clearly not divided into 29 books, but the divisions, almost always with incipits, correspond with the parts of Ivo's *Decretum*. For instance, Ivo's bk. IX, cap. 64 appears in its proper place as one of the canons under the heading *de incesta copulatione*, not as a separate book headed *de septem gradibus consanguinitatis*. On the other hand, headings have been put at the tops of the pages which do correspond with the headings of the 29 books given by Wasserschleben. So these MSS. are actually closer to their original than that described by Wasserschleben, and perhaps they represent an earlier form of the abridgment. Both MSS. have several folios missing at the end.

In pt. I the extracts from the first letter of Clement are followed by "Item Clemens in secunda ad Jacobum epistola", from which four extracts are given. Then comes "Clemens in secunda epistola sua", followed by six extracts, two of which had been given before. This looks like a revision. The total number of extracts from Clement is 29 as against 25 in

M. Fournier's MS.; so doubtless the first 4 extracts from Clement's second letter were omitted in the later recension. There are a number of other small variations in pts. I and II from the MS. described by M. Fournier. The scribe of the Caius MS. is sometimes rather careless. Thus after the extract from Euticianus in pt. I, the Oxford MS. goes on "Huic Gaius..."; in the Caius MS. this appears as "Huigarius".

(c) COLLECTIONS SIMILAR TO THE TRIPARTITA

MS.	Date	Provenance
1. B.M. Cotton. Cleopatra C. viii, ff. 64–91.	xii cent.	
2. B.M. Cotton. Vespasian A. xv.	xii cent.	Cirencester

I have said something about these in the text, where I gave reasons for thinking that no. I is not an abridgment from the *Tripartita*, but perhaps an earlier attempt which was later enlarged. Besides what I said then I may mention that a few canons of Councils are included which are not in the *Tripartita*. At any rate, if the scribe was definitely abstracting from the *Tripartita*, he must have been doing it with the sources in front of him. This MS. is mainly composed of canonical material. Folios 42–64 contain a mixed collection of canons, and there is another such collection, ff. 91–117. Folios 117ᵛ–125ᵛ contain the first two letters of Clement in full, and ff. 125ᵛ–135ᵛ a series of extracts from the Register of Gregory the Great, apparently taken consecutively from the 14 books.

No. 2, which has no introduction, is also apparently an independent compilation, but it is made from practically the same sources as those on which pt. I of the *Tripartita* depends. It starts off (f. 2) with "Clemens Jacobo in ea epistola. *Notum tibi facio*", and each letter is introduced in the same way with its address and incipit. There are 44, mostly quite short, extracts from Clement's first letter. The series of extracts from the False Decretals continues down to Gregory I (8 extracts). Then come (f. 67ᵛ) "Italius papa Paulo Cretensi episcopo...", (ff. 67ᵛ–71ᵛ) Martin of Braga, (f. 71ᵛ) "Martinus papa Amando...". Folios 71^v–77^v contain 25 extracts from the Boniface correspondence, quite different from the Selection in the *Tripartita*. Folios 77^v–130^v (where the MS. ends) contain extracts from Gregory I's Register, again differing from the *Tripartita*. In the middle of them (ff. 102 foll.) are interpolated a constitution of Charles, another of Carloman, and a few letters of Pope Boniface.

V. IVO OF CHARTRES

(Cf. P. Fournier, *Les collections canoniques attribuées à Yves de Chartres*, Bibl. de l'école des chartes, vols. LVII, LVIII. Paris, 1896–7.)

(a) THE DECRETUM IN 17 PARTS

(Ed. by Fronto, F. J., in *D. Ivonis Carnotensis episcopi opera omnia*. Paris, 1647. Reprinted in Migne, PL. CLXI.)

	MS.	Date	Provenance
1.	Corpus Christi Coll. Camb. 19.	xii cent.	Canterbury
2.	B.M. Royal, 11. D. vii.	xii cent.	Lincoln

The remarkable fact here is that each of these two important cathedral libraries possessed a copy of the *Decretum*, of which only five other copies are known in the whole of the rest of Europe.

(b) A COLLECTION IN 16 PARTS

(An abridgment of the *Decretum*, omitting pt. 17. Cf. P. Fournier, *op. cit.* vol. LVIII, pp. 412–413.)

1. B.M. Harleian, 3090.   xii cent.

This is in a foreign hand, and there is no evidence when it came into England. Only three other MSS. of this collection are known.

(c) THE PANNORMIA IN 8 BOOKS

(Ed. M. de Vosmediano in *Pannormia seu Decretum D. Ivonis Carnotensis episcopi*. Louvain, 1557. Reprinted in Migne, PL. CLXI.)

	MS.	Date	Provenance
1.	Jesus Coll. Oxford, 50.	xii cent., early.	
2.	B.M. Cotton. Vitellius, A. iii.	xii cent., 1st half	? Canterbury

MS.	*Date*	*Provenance*
3. Lincoln Cath. Lib. 192.	xii cent.	
4. Jesus Coll. Oxford, 26.	xii cent.	
5. St John's Coll. Oxford, 125.	xii cent.	
6. Hereford Cath. Lib. O. 6. xiii.	xii cent.	Hereford
7. Pembroke Coll. Camb. 103.	xii cent.	
8. Oxford. Bodl. Laud. Misc. 547.	xii cent.	
9. B.M. Add. 11,440 (3).	xii cent.	

I am only giving twelfth-century MSS. and of these the last two certainly do not seem to have been in England at that time. Only nos. 1 and 2 appear to belong to the first half of the century. No. 1, which seems the earliest and is written in a beautiful hand, is incomplete; it ends at bk. VI, cap. 117.

There are a number of MSS. of the thirteenth century, some of which are certainly foreign.

(*d*) A COLLECTION IN 10 BOOKS

(An enlargement of the *Pannormia*, of a peculiar kind. See P. Fournier, *op. cit.* vol. LVIII, pp. 433–442.)

1. Corpus Christi Coll. Camb. 94.	xii cent.	Canterbury

Only four other MSS. of this collection are known.

LIST OF MANUSCRIPTS
REFERRED TO

(*An asterisk denotes that only a small part of the MS is indicated in the description given of it. Page references are given in italic figures.*)

BRITISH MUSEUM

Cotton.   Claudius A. iii (*Lanfranc forgeries), *124 n.*
Cotton.   Claudius C. vi (Burchard), *89, 97, 237*
Cotton.   Claudius D. ix (Lanfranc's Collection), *63 foll.*, *231–5*
Cotton.   Claudius E. v (False Decretals), *66, 85–8, 97, 236*
Cotton.   Vitellius A. iii (Ivo, *Pannormia*), *244–5*
Cotton.   Vespasian A. xv (Collection of abstracts), *94, 243–4*
Cotton.   Vespasian E. iv (*re Peter's Pence), *182 n.*
Cotton.   Cleopatra C. viii (Collection of abstracts), *93, 243*
Cotton.   Faustina B. vi (*Lanfranc forgeries), *124 n.*
Royal, 9. B. xii (Lanfranc's Collection), *63 foll.*, *231–5*
Royal, 11. D. iv (False Decretals and Councils), *66, 86–7, 236*
Royal, 11. D. vii (Ivo, *Decretum*), *95, 97, 106, 244*
Royal, 11. D. viii (Lanfranc's Collection), *63 foll.*, *231–5*
Arundel, 173 (*Collection in 74 Titles*), *239–241*
Harleian, 633 (*Lanfranc's Collection—fragment), *81, 232*
Harleian, 3090 (A Collection in 16 parts), *95, 244*
Add. 11,440 (Ivo, *Pannormia*), *245*
Add. 22,286 (*Collection in 74 Titles*), *239–241*

CAMBRIDGE
University Library

Dd. i. 10, 11 (False Decretals), *66, 86, 236*

Corpus Christi College

19 (Ivo, *Decretum*), *95, 97, 244*
94 (A Collection in 10 Books), *95, 97, 245*
130 (Lanfranc's Collection), *63 foll.*, *231–5*
269 (Anselm of Lucca), *91, 241*
415 (Anonymous of York), *157*

Gonville and Caius College

455 (*Tripartita*), *93, 242–3*

Pembroke College

103 (Ivo, *Pannormia*—incomplete), *245*

Peterhouse

74 (Lanfranc's Collection), *63 foll.*, *97, 106, 162, 231–5*

ETON College Library

97 (False Decretals and Councils), *66, 77, 85–8, 236*

PARIS, Bibliothèque Nationale

Latin, 1563 (Lanfranc's Collection), *63 foll., 231–5*
· Latin, 3856 (Lanfranc's Collection, Pt. i), *63 foll., 231–5*
Latin, 6042 (Henry of Huntingdon), *103*

ROUEN

701 (Lanfranc's Collection, Pt. i), *63 foll., 231–5*
703 (Lanfranc's Collection, Pt. i), *63 foll., 231–5*

INDEX

Abbeville, Gilbert Foliot prior of, 197

Abbots, English, appointments of, 161, 167, 182–3, 188, 203; attitude of, to royal and papal authority, 160–1

Adrian I, Pope, 33

Adrian IV, Pope, 140 n.

African Church, Councils of, 61

Alberic, cardinal, papal legate to England, 102, 180–1

Albert, cardinal, papal legate to England, 10

Albinus, cardinal, *Provinciale* of, 16

Alexander II, Pope, 30, 42, 122–3, 126–7, 131 *n.*, 138, 161, 172, 185, 238; claim of, to William I, 141–3; letter to Lanfranc, 70, 75–6, 127, 232, 235

Alexander III, Pope, 7, 8, 10–11, 13, 20, 104, 197, 199, 209, 210, 216, 221–2; and the Becket controversy, 199, 202, 205–6, 208–10; decretals of, 128, 205, 213–4, 218, 223, 233; *Summa* of, 205

Alexander, bishop of Lincoln, 187

Anglo-Saxon, 49

"Anonymous of York", the, anti-papal attitude of, 157–8; supporter of royal authority in Church, 157, 159, 160

Anselm, St, archbishop of Canterbury, Chapter x, 5, 6, 10, 128–9, 134 n., 138, 145, 166, 170, 173–4, 178, 189; his early life, 147–9; character of, 126, 148–9; attitude of, to papal authority, 150–5, 160, 162–4, 190; and canon law, 149, 150; and primacy over York, 6, 172–3; and William II, 151–3; and Henry I, 151, 153–4, 162–3, 203; in exile, 153–4; Councils held by, 102, 170, 238

Anselm, bishop of Lucca, *Collectio Canonum* of, 37–9, 91, 241

Anselm, abbot of Sta Saba at Rome, papal legate to England, 168

Antherius, Pope, 74 n.

Antioch, Ecumenical Council at, 68–9

Aosta, 147

Arundel, Thomas, archbishop of Canterbury, 108

Assize Utrum, 204

Athanasius, St, 74

Atto, cardinal, *Capitulare* of, 37–8

Augustine, St, archbishop of Canterbury, 5, 177, 233 n.

Avranches, 215–6

Ayer, J. C., 16

Baldwin, archbishop of Canterbury, formerly abbot of Ford, 220; as papal legate, 218, 220; controversy with Christ Church, 11–12, 220, 224–5

Baldwin, abbot of St Edmund's Bury, 131 n.

Bari, Urban II's Council at (1098), 154 n.

Bartholomew, bishop of Exeter, a supporter of Becket, 196; *Penitentiale* of, 111–12

Bath and Wells, bishops of, and Glastonbury, 223

Bayeux, bishop of, *see* Odo

Beauvais, bishop of (Fulk), 159

Bec, abbey of, 57–8, 60, 65–6, 70, 76, 156; Lanfranc prior of, 118–9; Anselm prior and abbot of, 147–9; Theobald abbot of, 190; *see also* Libraries

Becket, St Thomas, archbishop of Canterbury, Chapter xiii, 7–10, 52, 110–11, 166–7, 169 n., 216, 219, 221; character of, 192–6, 208, 211; early training of, under archbishop Theobald, 190, 192, 194; as chan-

INDEX

253

Census, papal, 141, 143 n., 178, 184

Chalcedon, Ecumenical Council at, 159

Charlemagne, Emperor, 25, 33

Chartres, bishop of, *see* Ivo

Church, the, Chapters I–III *passim*; *ecclesia*, various meanings of, 15, 18–19; essential unity of, 23, 47; Church reform, 24 ff., 35, 38, 42, 100, 102, 128, 138, 146; centralisation of, under papal headship, 14, 28–30, 32, 36–9, 41, 43, 47, 72, 90–1, 99, 111, 117, 133, 139, 146–7, 157, 160, 172; *see* Papacy; *see also* English Church, France, Germany, etc.

Cirencester, priory of, *see* Libraries

Cistercian Order, 166, 184, 186

Civil Law, 34, 39, 57, 111, 118–9, 126, 197

Clarembald, abbot-elect of St Augustine's, Canterbury, 210

Clarendon, Constitutions of, 155, 167, 201–10, 212, 216, 228

Clement I, Pope, 60–1, 238, 242–3

Clement III, Pope, 15, 218

Clement III, anti-Pope (Wibert, archbishop of Ravenna), 71, 144–5, 152, 232

Clerical marriage, 25, 35, 48, 101, 128, 147, 158–9, 186

Clermont, Council at (535), 240; Urban II's Council at (1095), 104

Cluny, abbey of, 25; Customs of, 120; Gilbert Foliot monk and prior of, 197; Cluniac foundations, 184

Collection in 74 Titles, 37–9, 42, 92, 97; MSS. of, 90–1, 239–41

Compilationes of decretals, 107, 213–4

Corbett, W. J., 26

Councils, Church, share of, in canon law, 100–5; canons of, *passim*, and *see* Canon Law; collections of, *see* Chapters V, VI, Appendix. Ecumenical Councils, 33, 60–1, 80; *see also* Antioch, Chalcedon, Ephesus, Nicaea. Papal Councils, *see* Bari, Clermont, Rheims, Rome, Tours.

African Councils, 61. Gallican Councils, 61; *see also* Clermont, Orange, Orleans, Valence. Spanish Councils, 61; *see also* Elvira, Seville, Toledo. German Councils, *see* Mainz, Seligenstadt, Worms. English Councils, *see* London, Winchester, Windsor, York; *see also* English Church

Councils, royal, in England, *see* Pipewell, Rockingham, Winchester, Windsor

Criminous clerks, 200, 204–6, 212, 220

Dacheriana, the, 90 n., 91 n., 240 n.

Damasus I, Pope, 238

Decretales, of Gregory IX, 41, 98, 107–8, 213–4

Decretum, *see* Gratian; *see also* Burchard, Ivo

Denmark, 143 n.; *ecclesia Daciana*, 16

Deusdedit, cardinal, his canonical collection, 37–8, 141–3

Dionysio-Hadriana, the, 33, 50, 61, 68, 81, 90–1, 239

Dionysius, Pope, 74

Dionysius Exiguus, 33

Dunstan, archbishop of Canterbury, 49

Durham, cathedral, *see* Libraries; bishop of, *see* William of St Carileph

Eadmer, monk of Canterbury, author of *Historia Novorum* and Life of St Anselm, 80, 109, 121–2, 124, 134 n., 136–7, 147–8, 169, 203

Eastry, prior of Christ Church, Canterbury, 82, 98

Edward the Confessor, king of England, 23

Elvira, Council at, 67 n.

Ely, bishopric of, 78; bishop of, *see* William Longchamp

Empire, the, 14; and Papacy, 28, 118, 146, 157, 165; *see also* Germany

England, kingdom of, *passim*; claim of Papacy to subordina-

Roger, bishop of Salisbury, 187

Roger, bishop of Worcester, a supporter of Becket, 196

Roger of Howden, 103

Rome, 28, 127, 137–8, 153; Roman Church, *see* Papacy; Councils at, under Nicholas II (1059), 28, 65–6, 86, 127, 147, 240; under Gregory VII (1078), 240, (1080), 139; under Urban II (1099), 154; under Paschal II (1112), 233; under Calixtus II (First Lateran, 1123), 104, 169 n., 233, 238; under Innocent II (Second Lateran, 1139), 104, 179 n., 180 n.; under Alexander III (Third Lateran, 1179), 104; under Innocent III (Fourth Lateran, 1215), 100–1, 104

Rouen, archbishopric of, 139, 157–9; archbishops of, *see* John, William Bona Anima

Rudolf, anti-king of Germany, 140

St Albans, abbey, 120, 161

St Edmund's Bury, abbey, 107, 130–1, 185; *see also* Libraries; abbot of, *see* Baldwin

Salisbury cathedral, *see* Libraries; bishops of, *see* Jocelin, Osmund, Roger; *see also* John of Salisbury

Sta Saba, abbey, at Rome, abbot of, *see* Anselm

Savoy, 147

Scottish Church, *ecclesia Scoticana*, 15–17

Seligenstadt, Council at (1022), 238

Sens, archbishopric of, 139

Sergius I, Pope, 122

Seville, Council at, 60–1, 232; bishop of, *see* Isidore

Siegfried, archbishop of Mainz, 30, 42

Silvester, abbot of St Augustine's, Canterbury, 184

Simony, 25, 27, 35, 48, 65, 112, 128, 146–7, 162, 176, 184

Spain, Spanish Church, 37, 142, 172; Councils of, 61; *see also* Elvira, Seville, Toledo

Stenton, F. M., 187, 189 n.

Stephen, king of England, Chapter XII, 18, 165–6, 191, 194, 202, 205, 212, 227; Charter of, 4, 18–19, 176, 180, 184, 188, 206; relations of, with Papacy, 177, 179, 188–9; and English Church, 183–4, 187–8

Stephen Langton, archbishop of Canterbury, his election, 226; and Magna Carta, 4, 5, 20

Stigand, archbishop of Canterbury, 135

Stubbs, W., 100, 224

Sylverius, Pope, 68

Sylvester I, Pope, 60, 74

Teuzo, papal legate, 143 n.

Theobald, archbishop of Canterbury, 6, 8, 88, 110, 181, 183, 185, 192, 194–6, 199; as abbot of Bec, 190; as papal legate, 103, 182; holds legatine Council, 103; and study of canon law, 167, 189, 190; and papal authority, 177, 182, 189; his defiance of Stephen, 188, 194; his character and importance, 189, 190

Theoduin, cardinal, papal legate to England, 10

Thetford, bishopric of (later Norwich), bishops of, *see* Herbert Losinga, Herfast

Thomas, St, *see* Becket

Thomas I, archbishop of York, and the primacy of Canterbury, 125

Thomas II, archbishop of York, and contest with Canterbury, 6

Thurstan, archbishop of York, his success against Canterbury, 171

Tithes, held by laity, 25

Toledo, archbishop of, primate of Spain, 172; Councils at, 67 n., 68–9, 110, 150, 234

Tours, archbishopric of, 139; Alexander III's Council at (1163), 104

Tripartita (Collectio trium partium), 40, 52, 67, 92–4, 110–11, 242–4

Tudors, the, 20

260 INDEX

Urban I, Pope, 74, 81 n., 233
Urban II, Pope, 104, 148, 150–2, 154, 162, 172, 178, 238

Valence, Council at (855), 240
Victor III, Pope, 238
Victor III, anti-Pope, 199
Vitalian, Pope, 122

Waltham Abbey, *see* Libraries
Wasserschleben, H., 242
Wells, bishopric of, 156; bishop of, *see* Giso; *see also* Bath and Wells
Welsh Church, 16
Westminster, *see* London; abbey of, 161
Whitby, abbey, *see* Libraries; abbot of, *see* Richard
Wibert, archbishop of Ravenna, *see* Clement III, anti-Pope
William I (the Conqueror), king of England, Chapter IX, 25, 65, 120, 160, 169; as duke of Normandy, 26, 132; his Conquest, supported by Papacy, 134–5, 143, 180; and the English Church, 23–4, 26, 29, 56, 79, 126, 129, 132, 136–8, 140, 144, 151–2, 168, 172, 176, 200, 202–4; his control of appointments, 156; his relations with the Papacy, 27, 127, 129, 131 ff., 152–3, 163; and papal claim for fealty, 131, 140–4, 178; causes of his success, 146, 164–5
William II (Rufus), king of England, and the English Church, 26, 134 n., 145, 151–3, 161, 164–5; and the papal schism, 145, 152, 162, 178; and Anselm, 151–4; and Church reform, 160, 164–5; his view of royal authority, 145, 153, 165, 204

William de Corbeuil, archbishop of Canterbury, as papal legate, 102, 170, 173, 180; holds legatine Council, 102, 170, 238
William Bona Anima, archbishop of Rouen, 139, 158
William of St Carileph, bishop of Durham, 79, 109, 130, 145, 160–2, 204
William Longchamp, bishop of Ely, as papal legate, 218, 221; holds legatine Council, 218; as justiciar, 221
William Giffard, bishop of Winchester, 163
William FitzStephen, his life of Becket, 7
Winchester, William I's Council at (1072), 121, 123–4; cathedral church of, 120; Church Councils at (1070), 135, (1076), 102, 128; bishops of, *see* Henry of Blois, William Giffard
Windsor, William I's Council at (1072), 121; Church Council at (1070), 135
Wolsey, cardinal, 221
Worcester, bishopric of, 156, 223; bishops of, *see* Roger, Wulfstan; priory of, 80, 182 n.; prior of, *see* Nicholas; *see also* Libraries
Worms, Council at (868), 205 n.; bishop of, *see* Burchard
Wulfstan, bishop of Worcester, 80, 156

York, 12, 218; Council at (1195), 103; archbishops of, and contest with Canterbury, 5, 102, 124–6, 157, 159, 171–3; *see* Geoffrey, Roger, Thomas I, II, Thurstan; *see also* Anonymous of York